The C___
Fire-R___

'Mark!' shouted Jody. 'You can't go in there! You'll get killed!' Jody tried to hang on to Mark's arm, but he shook her off and disappeared into the crowd.

'Mark!' she shouted again, but her voice was drowned out by a cry from the crowd. The fire found a pocket of air, and suddenly a flame shot out of a first-floor window, forcing the fire fighters back.

Jody saw one fireman escape out of a window, half dragging and pushing a young man in front of him. The fireman had given his mask to the boy. The fireman staggered to the ground, overcome by smoke.

Jody saw Mark run up to the boy, throw his arms round him and lead him over to the side. The next thing Jody knew, an official-looking person was kneeling next to Mark, questioning him intensely . . .

Later, teenage gang leader Mark Brown, who had once before been charged with arson, was accused of starting the fire. But Jody was convinced someone was trying to frame him.

The third Jody and Jake Mystery

The Case of the Frightened Rock Star
The Case of the Counterfeit Racehorse

The Case of the Fire-Raising Gang

A Jody and Jake Mystery

Elizabeth Levy

KNIGHT BOOKS
Hodder and Stoughton

Copyright © 1981 by Elizabeth Levy

First published in the United States of America in 1981 by
Pocket Books, a Simon & Schuster division of
Gulf & Western Corporation, New York

First published in Great Britain by Knight Books 1982

British Library C.I.P.

Levy, Elizabeth
    The case of the fire-raising gang.
    I. Title
    823′.914[J]   PZ7

    ISBN 0-340-28585-0

Printed and bound in Great Britain for Hodder and Stoughton Paper-
backs, a division of Hodder and Stoughton Ltd, Mill Road, Dunton
Green, Sevenoaks, Kent (Editorial Office: 47 Bedford Square, London,
WC1 3DP) by Cox and Wyman Ltd, Reading. Photoset by Rowland
Phototypesetting Ltd, Bury St Edmunds, Suffolk

CONTENTS

1

FOLLOW THAT SIREN!

Jody heard the siren and immediately tensed. She was bicycling in high gear, zooming down a hill. She glanced behind her. The fire engine looked huge. She hugged the shoulder of the road, struggling to keep off the soft dirt. She didn't want to lose her balance. Her hands grabbed the handlebars so hard her knuckles turned white.

As the fire engine passed, Jody glanced up, catching the eye of a fireman clinging to the side of the engine. His face looked anxious. With his free hand he was struggling to pull up his long rubber boots to protect his thighs.

Jody felt the whoosh of air as the fire engine sped by. The siren was so loud she felt as if her eardrums would split. Finally she reached the bottom of the hill and she could slow down. She pulled over to the shoulder of the road and stood aside so that the next fire engine could go by.

Seconds later Jody's brother Jake came bicycling down the hill. 'Why did you stop?' he asked. 'Let's follow them.'

'I almost got run down by that fire engine,' complained Jody. 'They caught me on the downhill.'

'I heard them as I got to the corner,' said Jake, sounding eager. 'It sounds like a big fire.' Jake craned his neck and sniffed the air like a hound dog that had just picked up a scent.

'Forget it, Sparky,' said Jody. 'I'm not going to chase that engine. I've got a lot of homework.'

Ever since he was about nine Jake had been fascinated by fires and fire fighters. Whenever anyone asked him what he wanted to be, he always answered 'fireman'. Since his mother was a criminal lawyer and his father was a psychologist, nobody understood where Jake's desire came from. In fact, Jody often teased her younger brother that wanting to be a fire fighter was old-fashioned. But even now that he was fourteen Jake said that's what he would be when he grew up.

'Come on,' urged Jake. 'It sounds like it's close by. Let's find out what it is.'

'No,' said Jody, shaking her head. 'There's something ghoulish about chasing fires.'

'There is not,' protested Jake. 'It's a very respectable hobby. Remember that old guy, Arthur Fiedler, the conductor of the Boston Pops? He loved fires, and everybody loved him.'

'Yeah, well you are *not* a lovable old man!'

But Jake didn't listen to her. He took off on his bicycle, following the sound of the sirens. Jody considered going straight home, but her curiosity got the better of her.

As Jody and Jake rode closer to the fire they could see towers of black smoke spiralling in the air. 'It looks like it's in Northtown, near Vickers Stadium,' said Jake. Northtown was a rough neighbourhood, one that had been run-down for decades.

Jody saw the crowd gathered up ahead. Already almost a hundred people had gathered around the fire engines. Jake snaked his way through the crowd, and Jody lost sight of him. The wind changed and brought smoke into her face, a stinging, sweet odour. Jody looked at the burning building, an old three-storey house surrounded by a wooden verandah. The verandah was littered with broken glass, and Jody could see the fire fighters pulling their long hoses through the broken windows. Other fire fighters were directing their hoses towards the roof, trying to wet it down.

Jody was sorry she had come. She had more than her share of curiosity, but she never had been one to stop and stare at accidents. Jody hated to feel helpless. If she couldn't do anything to prevent something terrible from happening, then she didn't want to stand around and watch.

'I'm going home,' Jody muttered to herself. Jody started to push her way out of the crowd. She was almost knocked to the ground by a young man trying to push his way *towards* the fire.

'Let me through!' he demanded.

'Mark!' cried Jody.

Mark was a senior at Jody's high school. They weren't really friends. Mark hung out with a much rougher crowd than Jody's, but Jody had closer, more personal ties to Mark. Mark Brown had once been one of Jody's mother's clients. In fact, as Jody remembered with an awful feeling, the charge had been arson. Two years ago a fire had begun in an empty lot, but it spread to a neighbouring building. No one was hurt, but Mark admitted starting the fire. Mrs Markson had managed to keep him out of jail.

'What are you doing here?' Mark demanded. 'Slumming?'

Jody was stung by the bitterness in his voice.

'No!' she answered. 'Jake and I heard the sirens and came to see what was happening.'

'What's happening is my life is going up in smoke,' snapped Mark. At seventeen, Mark was a couple of years older than Jody, but he wasn't much taller than Jody's 5'6". He had short black hair – so dark it was almost blue-black – and deep-set eyes that made him look much older than

9

seventeen. Most teachers took an instant dislike to him. He walked with a kind of cocky, rolling gait. Only the bitter, set expression around his lips kept him from being handsome. He rarely joked around, and he was rumoured to have a terrible temper.

As Jody looked at Mark she could see big red blisters on his neck and hands. His clothes were full of soot. 'Mark!' she cried above the noise of the fire, 'did you get caught in the fire?'

'Worse,' said Mark. Jody didn't understand. Mark cursed under his breath and half shoved Jody aside.

'I've got to get in there,' Mark mumbled. 'I was working in there when suddenly I smelled smoke, and then the whole stair-well was on fire. I think David might still be in there. He was working in a back room. I got the rest of the kids out.'

'Mark!' shouted Jody. 'You can't go in there! You'll get killed!'

Jody tried to hang on to Mark's arm, but he shook her off and disappeared into the crowd. Jody tried to follow him, but she couldn't manoeuvre through the crowd with her bicycle.

'Mark!' she shouted again, but her voice was drowned out by a cry from the crowd. The fire found a pocket of air, and suddenly a flame shot out of a first-floor window, forcing the fire fighters back.

Jody saw one fireman escape out of a window, half dragging and pushing a young man in front of him. The fireman had given his mask to the boy. The fireman staggered to the ground, overcome by smoke. Other firemen quickly brought over an oxygen mask and forced it over his nose.

Jody saw Mark run up to the boy, throw his arms around him and lead him over to the side. The next thing Jody knew an official-looking person was kneeling next to Mark, questioning him intensely.

2

ALMOST A RIOT

'It's under control now,' Jake said to Jody, who had been staring so hard at Mark she hadn't realised Jake had come up behind her.

'Mark Brown must live here,' she whispered.

'Someone told me that it was an abandoned house,' said Jake. 'You must have heard wrong. Besides, I remember Mark lives on Delaware Avenue, a couple of blocks from here.'

'No,' said Jody. 'He was all excited. He said his whole life was going up in smoke. And he got burned. I could see the blisters on his hands.'

'Well, I asked around and I was told that the house was abandoned,' insisted Jake.

'Look,' said Jody, 'the police are questioning Mark. I wonder what's up.'

'Somebody said the fire looked suspicious,' said Jake. 'Didn't Mom get Mark off for arson a couple of years ago?'

'Yes,' said Jody. 'And he was proved innocent.'

'As I remember, he wasn't,' said Jake. 'I think Mom got him off on a technicality.'

'In this country you are supposed to be innocent until proved guilty,' snapped Jody.

'Hey,' said Jake, 'take it easy. You don't have to bite my head off.'

'I just hate it when people think someone is guilty just because they've been arrested before.'

'Hey,' said Jake, 'I'm not "people". I'm your brother, remember.'

'The police seem to be taking Mark away,' said Jody, ignoring Jake's comment. Two policemen half shoved Mark into a nearby police car.

'HEY! THE COPS GOT MARK!' shouted a girl about Jody's age. 'THE DIRTY PIGS!'

She ran forward and half threw herself on the police car. She pounded her fist on the windscreen. The girl looked back at the crowd.

'COME ON, YOU COWARDS, ARE YOU BULLETS OR NOT?' she screamed hysterically.

'Bullets?' whispered Jake. 'Let's get out of here. I don't want to get in the middle of a gang fight. This could get nasty.'

'Wait,' said Jody. A group of kids surged past her. They stopped and stared at the girl throwing herself against the police car. Inside the car the policeman was on his radio, obviously calling for help. The police and fire fighters were easily outnumbered by the crowd. Jody could sense that a riot might start any moment, yet she couldn't leave. She felt that if she stayed, maybe she would be able to do something.

'Okay, kids,' said one of the firemen, stepping forward. 'Everybody relax. It's been a tough day, but the fire's out.'

'DON'T LISTEN TO HIM!' shouted the girl. 'HE'S ONE OF THE PIGS TOO!'

'ONE OF THE PIGS?' shouted Jody, so angry she couldn't resist saying something. 'He just risked his life trying to save your neighbours.'

The girl was so surprised to hear another girl that she stopped pounding the police car.

'Who are you?' she demanded. 'You're not from the neighbourhood.' She turned towards Jody menacingly.

'Jody,' whispered Jake, 'this is a tough neighbourhood. Please, let's go.'

Meanwhile the gang of kids surrounding Jody seemed to get up their courage. A couple of them picked up loose bricks and pieces of timber.

'COME ON, MARK, GET OUT OF THE CAR,' shouted one of the boys.

'YEAH,' echoed another. 'LET HIM OUT ... OR ELSE.'

The fireman moved between the police car and the gang. 'The police just want to question him,' he urged. 'Mark will be back here in an hour or so.'

'Hey, what's with calling him Mark?' screamed the girl. 'Are you his best friend or something? Call him Mr Brown.'

Inside the police car Jody could see Mark talking urgently to the two policemen. He was nodding his head.

Then suddenly one of the bigger boys from the gang took a step forward and swung his piece of wood at the fireman. The fireman staggered back, blood running from his forehead. The gang started to surge forward towards the police car again, but Jody sensed that they were not really ready to riot. She felt that they were afraid, and reluctant to storm the police car, but the girl calling them cowards had embarrassed them.

The fireman wiped the blood from his forehead. He didn't seem seriously hurt. Then the rear door of the police car opened, and Mark stepped out, followed by one of the policemen.

He put his arm around the fireman and whispered something to him. The fireman nodded. Mark gave a disgusted look to the girl who was hanging on the police car.

'Get off there, Mary,' he said quietly.

She stared at him angrily, but she slowly pulled herself off the car.

'I don't want any firemen hurt,' said Mark, looking at the crowd. 'I want all the Bullets to make sure that the firemen are protected. We don't need a riot. The cops want to talk to me. I'll get a lawyer, but NO RIOT.'

Mark whispered something to the policeman standing next to him. The policeman nodded. Mark pointed to one of the kids holding a brick. He motioned the kid to come forward.

Mark stood huddled with the boy for several seconds. The boy was wearing a denim jacket with its sleeves ripped off. The name 'Bullets' was crudely written on the back of the jacket with a Magic Marker pen.

'I'm leaving Roy Washington in charge,' shouted Mark. 'He'll let me know who disobeys orders,' he warned.

Then Mark voluntarily opened the police car door and stepped in. He moved as if he owned the car and it was he who was in total control.

'Come on,' urged Jake. 'It could still get ugly. Let's go.'

Slowly the police car managed to inch down the street, and the crowd parted for it. Jody looked around for the girl who had started it all, but she seemed to have disappeared.

'Let's go,' repeated Jake.

'You were the one who wanted to watch the fire,' reminded Jody.

'I know,' said Jake, 'but I don't want to get in the middle of a gang war.'

'I think Mark cooled them off,' said Jody.

'Yeah,' said Jake, 'but he's not here any more to calm things down. I don't want to stick around to see if things flare up again.'

'Okay,' said Jody. She looked back at the half-burned house. Water was dripping down its sides, leaving ugly grey-black stains. Every window was broken. Inside Jody could see strands of insulation hanging from the ceiling, all curled and black from the flames. It didn't look like a place where anybody would ever live again.

3

MARK NEEDS A LAWYER

Jody unlocked the door to her own comfortable house at 918 Sullivan Street. Harpo, her mongrel with the tight, curly black hair of a poodle and the long floppy ears of a spaniel, greeted her at the door as if he hadn't seen her in years. Chico and Groucho, the Marksons' two cats, sauntered over and leisurely rubbed against Jody's legs, yet managed to act as if they looked down on Harpo's open display of affection.

'A scene like that makes you realise how lucky we are, doesn't it?' said Jake.

'You know, that's exactly what I was thinking,' said Jody. 'We take it so for granted. If we had been born to different parents, we could be living in a slum, too.'

'Yeah, but you would probably be living in a neat slum,' said Jake. Jody was notoriously neat. She took after her father, not her mother.

'Are you cooking tonight?' asked Jody.

Jake nodded. Jake was by far the best cook in the Markson family. Jody could follow a recipe exactly, and the food would turn out all right. Jake would take a glance at the same recipe, and somehow the food tasted wonderful. His speciality was all kinds of pasta.

Jake went into the kitchen to begin dinner. Because Mrs

Markson worked so hard and such long hours, Jody and Jake were responsible for most of the cooking. When Mrs Markson took over for dinner, they usually had pizza or Chinese food take-away.

'I can't get that fire out of my mind,' said Jody, absent-mindedly munching on a carrot Jake had just peeled.

'Hey,' said Jake, 'that's for my sauce. If you want a carrot, peel your own.' And he handed Jody an unpeeled carrot.

'What are you making?' asked Jody.

'Bolognese sauce,' said Jake. 'It looks just like regular spaghetti sauce, but it's got everything in it. Even chicken livers.'

'Yuk!' exclaimed Jody.

'Wait till you taste it,' said Jake.

First Jake took some strips of bacon and put them in a frying-pan over a low flame, and then he added some strips of ham. Just then Mrs Markson came into the kitchen.

'It smells delicious,' she said, taking a deep sniff. Mrs Markson had a well-fed look, mostly due to Jake's cooking.

'That's because he hasn't put in the yukky chicken livers,' said Jody.

'Just wait,' said Jake. 'Hi, Mom.'

'Hi, kids. How was your day?'

'Mom, did you hear about the fire?' asked Jody.

'What fire?' asked Mrs Markson.

'There was a fire on Thornton Street by Vickers Stadium,' said Jody. 'Mark Brown was somehow involved.'

'Mark?' repeated Mrs Markson, frowning. She looked very concerned. 'What did he have to do with it?'

'He said it was his house,' answered Jody.

'He doesn't live there. He lives in the housing project on Delaware Avenue,' said Mrs Markson.

'That's what I said,' interjected Jake, stirring his sauce.

'Anyhow,' continued Jody, 'there was almost a riot when the police took Mark in for questioning.'

'WHAT!?' exclaimed Mrs Markson.

'The police made Mark get into their police car,' said Jody.

'Oh no,' sighed Mrs Markson. 'I hope he's not in trouble again.' She looked up. 'How did you happen to be in that neighbourhood anyway?' she asked sharply.

'You know Sparky,' said Jody. 'We were biking home from school when we heard the sirens, and Jake couldn't resist following the fire engines.'

'I keep telling you that liking to watch fire fighters is a perfectly respectable hobby. It doesn't make me into some kind of firebug or anything.'

Mrs Markson smiled affectionately. 'I know,' she said. 'It's just that I always thought it was a phase you were going through. I remember when you were five years old, your Uncle George gave you a fireman's hat, and you wouldn't take it off. You were the palest kid in kindergarten because you would never go outside without your fire hat.'

Jake laughed. 'Maybe I was just smart and knew I would never get a tan anyhow.' With red hair and pale skin Jake had basically two different colours – pale white or lobster red. If he went out in the sun he burned, peeled and then burned again.

'Yeah, but red-heads look terrible in red,' said Jody. 'You don't look good in a fire hat.'

'You're just still jealous because Uncle George didn't bring you one,' said Jake. 'He probably brought you a doll.'

Mrs Markson's brother had very old-fashioned ideas about what girls should be like. He had never really got over the fact that his own sister had turned out to be a prominent criminal lawyer.

Just then the phone rang, and Jody picked it up. She

listened for a moment and then asked anxiously, 'Are you all right?'

'Who is it?' whispered Mrs Markson.

Jody mouthed the word 'Mark'. Then she said, 'Just a minute,' and handed the phone to her mom.

'What did he say?' asked Jake.

'The police are letting him call a lawyer,' said Jody.

'That doesn't sound good,' said Jake. 'I guess they think it's arson.'

'It's not fair!' exclaimed Jody. 'I bet they just picked on him because of that old charge.'

Mrs Markson hung up the phone. 'I've got to go to the police station. I told Mark not to answer any questions until I get there.'

'Do the police think Mark started the fire?' asked Jody.

'Mark wasn't making much sense,' said Mrs Markson. 'I'll find out more when I get there. Start dinner without me.'

'Don't worry,' said Jake. 'This is a sauce that keeps . . . we'll be eating it for days.'

Mrs Markson looked distracted.

'Mom, are you okay?' asked Jody. 'You look upset.'

Mrs Markson ran her hand through her daughter's long hair, and brushed it behind her ear. 'I'm fine,' she said. 'It's just that two years ago, I put myself out on a limb because I believed in Mark. If it turns out that he really did start that fire, then I'm partially responsible. I'm the one who got him off.' Mrs Markson picked up her car keys and left.

Jody stared after her. 'He's not guilty,' she whispered. 'I know it.'

'Uh-oh,' murmured Jake.

'What does that mean?' demanded Jody.

'Nothing,' said Jake. 'Only, when you get that tone in your voice, I know you and I are going to be in the middle of it.'

'Oh, go stir your spaghetti sauce,' said Jody impatiently.

4

OUT ON BAIL

Jody and Jake ate their dinner in silence. They were used to eating dinner alone when Mrs Markson worked late on a case, but usually they chatted and teased each other all through the meal. Jake didn't like it when Jody was so quiet.

Jody wound her spaghetti around her fork and stared at it absent-mindedly for a second. Then she put down her fork.

'Is something wrong with it?' asked Jake.

'No,' said Jody shortly.

'You looked at it as if it were worms, not spaghetti,' said Jake, sounding hurt.

Jody looked up. She realised that she and her mom tended to take Jake's hard work in the kitchen for granted. 'It's delicious,' she said. 'I'm just not hungry. That fire made me lose my appetite. I wish Mom would come home so we could find out what happened to Mark.'

'Why this sudden interest in Mark?' asked Jake. 'He's not exactly your type.'

There were over four hundred kids in Jody and Jake's high school, but Mark could have lived in a completely different world as far as Jody's friends were concerned. Despite nearly failing grades, Mark managed to stay in school, but almost all of his gang were drop-outs. Almost all of Jody's friends were in the top ten per cent.

In fact, Jody would probably never even have spoken to Mark if her mother hadn't happened to have been his lawyer. Most of Jody's friends didn't even realise Jody knew Mark.

Once again Jody's mother was involved. Only this time, instead of being a thirteen-year-old kid with braces, Jody was fifteen, and she had some experience helping her mother with her cases and investigating cases on her own. Jody wondered whether she'd be able to help this time.

'Look,' said Jake, 'I don't mind eating alone, but I hate to do it with a zombie sitting next to me.'

'I'm sorry,' said Jody. 'I was just daydreaming. I think I've had enough.'

'What's up?' asked Jake. 'The fire shouldn't have made you that upset. Nobody was killed.'

'I know,' said Jody. 'I just feel bad whenever I'm in Northtown. People shouldn't have to live like that. I wish there was something we could do.'

'Mom does more than most,' said Jake. 'She takes on a lot of clients who can't pay. Most of them are from Northtown.'

'But that's something *Mom* does, not us,' said Jody. 'We should be doing something ourselves.'

'Well, right now I'd better do my homework,' said Jake, 'or I'm gonna be a drop-out myself.' Jake was not a great student. He was good at English and history, subjects he liked, but he was terrible at maths and science.

Jody, on the other hand, was a consistent grade-A student. She got *A*'s in maths and she got *A*'s in English. Jake got *A*'s in English because his papers were so funny his teachers forgave him the fact that he couldn't spell. Jody's papers were usually less creative, but she never misspelled a word. When Jody was ten she had come in second in a statewide spelling bee.

Jody cleared the table and went up to her room to do her own homework. Jody needed complete silence when she studied. Jake claimed that he couldn't study without the radio on. Last Christmas Jody had given him a headset for his stereo.

At around nine-thirty Jody heard her mother's car in the driveway. Jody's bedroom window looked over their front garden. She looked out as her mother swung open the door on the driver's side and leaned back into the car to say something to a person sitting in the passenger seat. Mrs Markson seemed to be arguing with the person. Then she grabbed her briefcase and walked around the car. Seconds later Jody saw someone get out of the passenger seat. He walked towards the front door with his head hanging down but Jody knew it was Mark. Suddenly he turned to say something to Mrs Markson. The street-light shone on his jacket, and Jody could read 'Bullets'. Unlike the other gang members, Mark's jacket had embroidered sequins spelling out his own name and then the name 'Bullets'. Jody wondered who had taken the trouble to do the embroidery. Somehow she couldn't picture Mark doing the work himself.

Jody ran to the mirror and quickly brushed her hair and put on lip gloss. Then she ran downstairs.

'Hi, Mom!' she said, as her mom opened the door. 'Oh, Mark,' said Jody, pretending surprise, 'I didn't realise you were here. I just heard Mom's car in the driveway and came downstairs.'

'We couldn't get hold of Mark's dad,' said Mrs Markson. 'I had to arrange bail, and I wanted Mark to come here until we find his dad.'

'Dad and I had a fight,' said Mark. 'He could be anywhere.'

'Then you're staying here until we find him,' said Mrs Markson. She sounded angry. Jody stood on the stairs, not knowing exactly **what to do**. Mark looked exhausted. His clothes were still full of soot and ash from the fire.

'Come in and let's have some dinner,' said Mrs Markson. She threw her briefcase down on the hall table and took off her coat. 'There's some spaghetti left, isn't there?' she asked.

'I'm sure,' said Jody. 'I'll heat it up.'

Jody went into the kitchen. She had just put Jake's sauce back on the stove when Jake came storming into the kitchen.

'What are you doing?' he asked.

'Fixing Mom and Mark some dinner,' said Jody. 'What's the problem?'

'Nothing,' said Jake, 'but you put that sauce on a high flame. You'll burn it up.'

'Well, *I* was in a hurry,' complained Jody.

'You'll ruin my sauce. Anyhow, what's wrong with Mom? I came downstairs to say hi, and she practically snapped my head off.'

'I have a feeling she and Mark are having a fight,' said Jody. 'I don't know what it's about.'

'Well, they're in the living room,' said Jake. 'You go in and find out, and I'll bring them dinner.'

'Thanks,' said Jody. As she was about to leave the kitchen she turned. 'Why do you want me to find out what happened?' she asked.

'Because I can tell that something's got you worked up. I told you I figure I'm going to be in the thick of it anyway. I might as well find out what to look out for.'

'You don't have to get involved,' said Jody.

'I know,' said Jake. 'And neither do you, but do you want to make any bets about whether we get involved or not?'

'Nope,' agreed Jody, and she went into the living room.

5

'HE'S GONE!'

Mark sat on the edge of the couch. The cats, Chico and
Groucho, stood on the floor, staring at him as if unsure
whether to approach him. Finally Groucho jumped up on
Mark's lap. Without thinking, Mark brushed Groucho off,
sending him tumbling to the floor.

Mrs Markson sat at her desk, making a phone call. 'Still no
answer,' she said. She turned and saw Jody. 'Is dinner
ready?' she asked.

'Jake's heating it up,' answered Jody. 'Mark, can I get you
a soda or anything?'

Mark shook his head.

Mrs Markson looked at him. 'Mark, it's silly for you to stay
in those clothes. Why don't you take a shower and get Jake to
lend you something to wear?'

'I'm all right,' mumbled Mark.

'I know,' said Mrs Markson, 'but your clothes stink of the
fire and of jail. *I'm* sick of the smell. Go find Jake and get him
to help you.'

Mark sighed, pushed himself off the couch and left the
room. Mrs Markson watched him go and then sighed herself.

'Mom,' asked Jody, 'is Mark in bad trouble?'

'Yes,' said Mrs Markson wearily. 'The worst. The prosecutor had the choice of treating him as a juvenile or as an adult. Mark's seventeen, and arson is a serious crime. The judge decided to treat Mark as an adult. That means he could get ten years in prison. That's prison. Not a juvenile detention home. I feel sick about it.'

'But how come the police picked Mark up so fast?' asked Jody. 'I was at the fire. The fire was barely out when the police were questioning Mark. It seemed way too soon for them to have made an investigation, much less an arrest.'

Mrs Markson smiled. 'You are going to make a great lawyer someday. Naturally the same question occurred to me. Apparently, at the same time someone phoned in the fire alarm, they gave the fire department a tip that the fire had been started by Mark. They even told the police where to look for the paraffin cans. They were in a pile of rubble outside the house. They brought Mark in for questioning, and later they found one of the cans had Mark's fingerprints on it.'

'It sounds like he was set up,' said Jody. 'Did the person giving this information leave a name?'

'No,' said Mrs Markson. 'It was an anonymous tip, but the police solve many cases through anonymous tips. Just because the person didn't want to leave his or her name doesn't necessarily mean he or she was lying.'

'But you believe they were lying, don't you?' asked Jody.

'As Mark's lawyer, of course I'll try to prove it's a lie,' said Mrs Markson. 'But frankly, and this can't go outside of the room, I don't know what to believe. Mark won't talk to me. He'll have to before the trial, but he has hardly said ten words to me.'

'But Mom,' protested Jody, 'you thought Mark was innocent the last time.'

'No, not innocent,' said Mrs Markson softly. 'I thought that he shouldn't be punished. Those are two very different things, and this time it seems quite different. For one thing, Mark was much younger then. Also, he was going through a very difficult time. His parents were just getting a divorce; it got ugly, and Mark was caught in the middle. He admitted to starting the fire in the empty lot. He wanted attention and he got it. They've made a study of children who start fires. Most are boys and most come from homes in which there have been recent changes – a death, a divorce, even a new baby. All can cause certain children to start playing with fire. I remember I met a very nice young fire fighter when I was working on Mark's case. Ben Walker was his name. He took Mark under his wing and gave him some counselling. The fire fighters have a very good community relations programme, and he was a terrific man. He helped me understand arson and why kids play with fire.'

'Did I start a fire when Jake was born?' asked Jody.

Mrs Markson laughed. 'You were only a year and a half old. You were a precocious child, but not that precocious. However, once you did yell at me to take Jake back to the store. You wanted him to return like a piece of defective merchandise.'

'Who are you calling defective merchandise?' asked Jake.

'You,' said Jody. 'Mom was telling me that when you were born I told her to return you to the store.'

'Thanks,' said Jake. 'I always suspected you wanted to be an only child.'

'Only sometimes,' said Mrs Markson. 'Actually, Jody was fascinated with you as a baby. Sometimes I think she taught you more than your dad or I did.'

'Maybe that's why I talk funny. Yuk, yuk,' said Jake.

'Yuk, yourself,' said Jody.

'Is Mark taking a shower?' interrupted Mrs Markson.

'Yup,' said Jake. 'I showed him where it was, and I lent him some clothes. Anyhow, your dinner is ready.'

'Thanks, honey,' said Mrs Markson. 'Why don't you go up and knock on the bathroom door and tell Mark it's time to eat.' Mrs Markson looked at her watch. 'It's ten o'clock already,' she said. 'No wonder I'm starved.'

Mrs Markson walked into the kitchen, and Jody followed her. Her mother's words disturbed her. Often Mrs Markson discussed her cases with Jody and Jake. They had learned from an early age how to keep a secret. But Jody knew that her mother was normally a very optimistic lawyer. Even when everyone might think her client guilty, Mrs Markson usually found a good reason to believe he or she was innocent.

Mrs Markson said that it didn't matter whether her clients were guilty or innocent. They deserved someone fighting for them, and that was her job. Sometimes Mrs Markson called herself a 'hired gun'. But Jody knew that one of the reasons Mrs Markson was so successful as a lawyer was that very often she truly believed in her client's innocence. The juries could sense that Mrs Markson was more than a hired gun.

Now Jody was worried. Mrs Markson had rarely sounded so discouraged. It wasn't like her. Jody knew that two years ago Mrs Markson had truly gone out on a limb to keep Mark out of a juvenile detention home. Mark wasn't just a case to her. Now Jody wasn't sure Mrs Markson had faith in Mark, not just in his innocence, but as someone who was worthwhile, worth fighting to help.

Suddenly Jake came running into the kitchen. He was holding a damp towel. 'He's gone!' said Jake. 'He isn't down here, is he?'

'No,' said Mrs Markson sharply, sucking in her breath. 'What do you mean "gone"?'

'I went upstairs and I heard the shower running,' said Jake. 'I knocked on the door to tell him to hurry up 'cause his dinner was ready, and he didn't answer. I knocked again, and when he still didn't answer I opened the door, figuring that he couldn't hear me over the shower. At first the room was so steamed up I couldn't see anything, but then I realised there was nothing behind the shower curtain.'

'Was he in your room?' asked Jody. 'Maybe he had gone there to change his clothes.'

'Nope. It's like the phantom,' said Jake. 'All he left was a wet towel.'

'He'd better not have gone far,' said Mrs Markson. 'His bail is good only if he doesn't leave the jurisdiction. If he skips bail, I'll never forgive myself.'

'Mark wouldn't do that,' said Jody. 'He must have had a good reason for leaving without telling us.'

6

GANGS AND SISSIES

At school the next day Jody stood by her locker, waiting to see if she could get a glimpse of Mark.

'Come on,' urged her best friend, Robie. 'We'll be late for class.'

'You go on,' said Jody. 'I remembered I left a notebook in the science room. I have to get it.'

'I'll come with you,' said Robie, good-naturedly.

Jody frowned. She hadn't left a notebook. She just happened to know that Mark had science the next period, and she wanted to see if he had come to school.

'No reason for us both to be late,' said Jody. 'Why don't you go and tell Mr MacDonald I'm coming.'

'If we stop talking about it we can both be there,' said Robie. 'What's wrong with you today? You've been acting queerly.'

'I'm sorry,' said Jody. She didn't want to tell Robie what had happened last night, but she hadn't realised she had been so preoccupied.

Robie followed Jody to the science room. The senior's class was just settling down. Jody looked in. Mark was standing in the back talking to a Bullet, David Ruggerio. He glanced up and gave Jody a guilty look.

'Where's your notebook?' asked Robie.

'Uh . . . someone must have picked it up for me,' mumbled Jody. 'Come on, let's go to our class.'

Robie and Jody ran down the hall to their class and made it just as the bell was ringing.

As she slid into her seat all of Jody's books fell to the floor. Mr MacDonald gave her an annoyed look. Robie bent down to help Jody pick up her books. She picked up one notebook and stared at it.

'Hey!' whispered Robie. 'You had your science notebook all along. What's going on?'

''I'll tell you later,' whispered Jody.

'Ms Markson,' said Mr MacDonald dryly, 'would it be all right with you if we started class?'

'I'm sorry,' said Jody.

At the end of class Robie cornered Jody out in the hall. 'Why did we go on that wild-goose chase for your notebook?'

'I just had to see if Mark Brown was in school,' said Jody.

'Mark Brown!' said Robie. 'What do you have to do with him? You know he's the gang leader of the Bullets. He's bad news.'

'He is not,' protested Jody.

'Mark Brown,' said another of their classmates as they overheard Mark's name. 'He's in bad trouble. I hear the police arrested him for arson in that fire near Vickers Stadium.'

'Is that true?' said Robie. 'Then what's he doing in school?'

'He's on bail,' said Jody indignantly. 'He's got a perfect right to be in school. He's not guilty until he has a trial and the jury convicts him. I don't know why I have to keep reminding everyone.'

'Isn't that cute?' said a voice behind Jody. 'Mark has got himself a junior defender.'

Jody whirled around. She found herself face to face with Joey Hennessey, another senior from Northtown, but Joey was the gang leader of the Razors.

'What's the matter?' taunted Joey. 'Did the great Mrs Markson have too many clients? Did she have to start giving them to her daughter?'

'My mom's clients are no business of yours,' said Jody angrily.

'Right,' laughed Joey. 'Only I bet she's not going to have an easy time getting Mark off this time. Of course, with *you* helping . . .' Joey poked Jody in the arm playfully, only his poke hurt.

'What's going on?' asked Jake as he came by on his way to the lunch room. By this time a fair number of people had gathered around.

'Nothing,' said Jody. 'Let's go, Robie. We have to get to the lunch room too.'

'What's the matter?' asked Joey. 'Are you afraid to be seen with the Razors? I guess you only like gangs made up of sissies, like the Bullets. Sissies who like to play house.'

'Let's go,' said Jody again. She had never liked Joey Hennessey, but at least he had always ignored her.

Just then a group of Bullets walked down the hall.

'Hey,' shouted a Razor, 'here come the sissies.'

Mark came up to the group. He seemed disturbed to see Jody talking to Joey Hennessey.

'Oh . . . hi, Mark,' said Joey, suddenly sounding a lot less tough. He looked around and seemed to realise that the Razors were outnumbered.

Mark ignored him. He looked at Jody. 'I'm sorry about last night,' he said.

'Well now,' sneered Joey, 'isn't that sweet? I bet Mary will be interested in hearing that her old boyfriend has suddenly gone for the brainy type.'

Jody blushed.

'Mind your own business, Joey,' said Mark, but he looked embarrassed, as if he realised that he had said the wrong thing.

'Sure, sure,' said Joey. 'I guess you have a good reason to date your lawyer's daughter.' And he turned and sauntered off down the hall.

Jody felt so embarrassed she wanted to die.

Even Mark seemed flustered. 'I'm sorry,' he said.

'That's okay,' said Jody, hugging her books and looking down at her notebooks as if they held important secret information.

'Was Joey bothering you?' Mark asked.

Jody shook her head no. 'He was just teasing me. It's okay.' Jody looked at Robie. She wished she would leave. She knew she had to talk to Mark alone. She gave Robie a little signal with her head. Robie just stared at Mark as if she couldn't believe she was actually talking to the gang leader of the Bullets. Finally Jody nudged her with her foot.

'Oh,' said Robie, finally getting the point. 'I've got to go to the lunch room. Jody, I'll save you a place.'

'Thanks,' said Jody. She smiled at her friend gratefully.

'Right,' said Robie. 'We'll have plenty to talk about,' she said meaningfully.

Jody turned to Mark. 'How could you just run out of our house last night?' she asked accusingly. 'Mom was so upset she didn't know what to do.'

'I called her this morning to apologise. I just couldn't stay in your house. I got the shakes. I had to get out.'

'Why?' asked Jody.

'I don't have to explain myself to you,' snarled Mark.

Jody took a step back, surprised by Mark's outburst. She looked into his deep eyes. He sounded so bitter and angry. She thought about their home on Sullivan Street, the dog and cats, Jake's cooking, the love and security. Suddenly she could understand why Mark might not have been able to stand it. Jody believed the contrast between the Marksons' home and Mark's own was too great, especially on the night that all of his dreams for a better home had gone up in smoke.

7

INTRODUCING FANG

After school Robie cornered Jody and Jake at the bike stand. 'Would you mind telling me when you started messing around with the Bullets and the Razors?' she demanded. 'They are more than a little scary.'

'I am not messing around,' protested Jody.

'Well, they're a little tough for my blood,' said Robie.

Jody unlocked her bicycle.

'Where are you going?' asked Robie.

'To Northtown,' answered Jody.

'Did I hear you right?' asked Robie. 'You're going to Northtown? Why?'

'I want to see that building that burned yesterday,' said Jody.

'Why?' repeated Robie.

'Because Mark isn't telling anybody what's really going on, and we need to find out if Mom is going to defend him.'

'*If* is the big question,' said Jake. 'After the way Mark ran out on her yesterday, I wonder whether she's still his lawyer.'

'He said he called to apologise,' said Jody, 'and I think I understand why he left.'

'I don't think Jody should go to Northtown by herself,' said Robie worriedly.

'I'll be fine,' said Jody. 'You sound like a mother hen.'

'I'll go with you,' said Jake.

'Well, if Jake is going, I'll go too,' said Robie.

'We don't have to travel as a gang,' said Jody.

'Why not?' asked Jake. 'Everyone else in that neighbour-hood does. Let's see, there's the Bullets and the Razors; maybe we should call ourselves the Pillows.'

'Pillows?' repeated Jody.

'Yeah, 'cause we're the obvious softies,' said Jake.

'Speak for yourself,' said Robie, who was one of Shady Brook's track stars, specialising in the eight hundred metres.

Jody, Jake and Robie rode their bikes to Northtown. Every once in a while, among the burned out and dilapidated build-ings, they would see a spruced-up house, freshly painted.

'You know, there are some nice houses around here,' said Robie.

Just then a large dog bounded down the street, snarling at them and barking furiously. The dog startled Robie and she swerved, hitting the curbstone.

'Help!' she cried as she lost her balance and fell to the street.

Jody and Jake both braked and charged towards the dog, who was hovering over Robie and growling menacingly. Jody pretended to pick up a rock and made a throwing motion at the dog. The dog flinched, but didn't run away.

'Don't show fear,' Jody said in a whisper to Robie.

'Too late. I think I've shown it,' whispered Robie. 'Get that dog away from me.'

Suddenly they heard a girl's voice laughing. 'That-a-boy, Fang,' said the girl.

Jody whirled around to see Mary Aurelio, Mark's old girlfriend, the girl who had almost started the riot the day before.

'Call off your dog,' said Jody quietly.

Mary laughed. 'He's just protecting the neighbourhood.'

'Please,' whispered Robie, as the dog continued to snarl above her.

Jody advanced towards the dog. He turned his attention away from Robie and watched Jody. He growled deep in his throat, his tail hung down, and the fur on his throat stood up. 'Easy, Fang, easy,' crooned Jody. She extended her hand with her fingers curled inwards to show Fang that she wasn't about to grab him or hit him.

Fang sniffed at her hand, his curiosity aroused at the possibility that there might be some food in Jody's hand. Very slowly, his tail began to wag back and forth. 'That-a-boy,' whispered Jody. 'See, you're not such a terrible fellow.'

Fang took another step forwards. His tail was wagging, his mouth hung open in the semblance of a smile. Jody patted him on the back. 'Good boy,' she said.

'Come here, Fang,' demanded Mary. Fang looked up and obediently padded to Mary's side.

'That's quite a dog you've got there,' said Jake.

'Yeah,' said Mary, 'he's good protection. We don't like it when kids like you come slumming.'

'We're not slumming,' said Jody, watching as Robie scrambled back on her bike.

'Oh no?' said Mary. 'What are you doing here then?'

'We wanted to find out more about the fire yesterday,' said Jody.

'What do *you* have to do with that?' asked Mary angrily.

'Mark is my mother's client,' said Jody.

'Yeah, well, I guess he needs a woman lawyer, now that he's turned the Bullets into such sissies,' answered Mary.

'That's the second time someone's called the Bullets sissies,' said Jody. 'Why?'

'Because Mark has turned them into little home-bodies,' said Mary. 'Everyone thinks it's so cute the way they are fixing up the neighbourhood. If you ask me, they're just looking for brownie points.'

'I don't understand,' said Jody.

'Yeah, well, you're the all-time super-achiever,' said Mary. 'You spend your whole life chalking up brownie points.'

'I do not!' protested Jody.

'Besides,' said Jake, 'what's so bad about being a super-achiever?' He knew that Mary was rumoured to be close to dropping out of school.

'All this is beside the point,' said Jody. She didn't want to get into a fight with Mary. She knew Mary could give them valuable information if only she would trust them.

'Look, Mary,' she said, 'I know you and Mark were friends. You must have some feelings left for him. I only want to help him too.'

Mary looked at Jody suspiciously. 'You've been listening to old gossip,' said Mary. 'Mark and I broke up. I broke up with him about a month ago, right about the time he got so hipped up on his "rehabilitation" project, trying to get all the kids in the gang to go along with him.' Mary practically spat on the ground. 'I told you, he's turned into a sissy . . . a little do-gooder.'

'Mark, a do-gooder!' exclaimed Jake. 'That's not exactly his reputation.'

'Well, that shows you how much you know,' said Mary. 'Come on, Fang. We're wasting our time.' Mary turned her back on them and coolly walked down the street.

'She's certainly friendly,' said Jake sarcastically.

'Can you imagine calling a dog Fang?' said Jody. 'The poor dog has everybody afraid of him, even if he's got the nicest personality in the world.'

'If you ask me, Fang's name fits his personality,' said Robie.

8

THE FRONTIER SPIRIT

'What a mess!' exclaimed Robie as they stood in front of the burned-out hull. The house was still standing, but the walls were charred, and everything had a soggy, sooty look.

'It doesn't look like anyone will ever live here again,' said Jody.

But from inside the house they heard the sound of hammering. 'Someone's inside,' said Jake.

'Let's go,' said Jody. She walked up the steps of the verandah. One of the steps was completely burned through.

'It looks dangerous,' said Jake. 'I don't know if we should go walking through here.' He looked around at all the broken glass scattered on the verandah.

Jody ignored him. The door had been completely destroyed by the fire fighter's axe. It hung in pieces from the hinges. Jody stood in the doorway and peered into the house. The bright, sunny day made the soggy pieces of plasterboard and exposed wiring look even more pitiable.

'Is anybody home?' Jody shouted.

'This doesn't look like a home,' whispered Jake.

A boy about the same age as Jody came out. He was wearing a cut-off denim jacket with 'Bullets' marked on the back. Jody recognised him as the boy Mark had left in charge just before the police had taken him away.

'What are you doing here?' he asked suspiciously.

'Is Mark Brown here?' Jody asked.

'Who wants him?' asked the boy. He held the hammer in his hand and he rhythmically pounded it into his fist.

'I'm Jody Markson. My mom is defending Mark,' answered Jody.

The boy didn't seem impressed. 'Who told you Mark would be here?' he asked.

'Nobody,' answered Jody. She didn't like being so closely questioned, especially without getting a chance to ask any questions of her own. 'Did you live here?' she asked.

'Why do you want to know?' sneered the boy.

'I just don't understand why the Razors are calling you sissies,' said Jody. 'Is it because you're fixing up this house?'

The boy raised his hammer in his hand and swung it in the air. 'Hey, some Razors are here calling us sissies,' he shouted.

'We're not Razors and we didn't call you sissies,' protested Jody.

Suddenly from the back of the house about five other kids appeared. They, too, had on cut-off denim jackets with 'Bullets' stencilled on the back. All the kids were covered with grey ash and looked as if they had been working.

'What's going on, Roy?' asked one of the boys.

'These kids just showed up,' said Roy. He pointed his hammer at Jody. 'She says she's the daughter of Mark's lawyer, but I don't know what they're doing down here. They could be Razor spies.'

'They don't look like Razors,' said one kid.

'That's because they're spies, dummy,' said Roy.

'Let's get out of here,' whispered Jake. 'I don't feel like staying around for a spy trial.' Jody ignored him.

'We came to try to help Mark,' said Jody.

'He doesn't need your help,' snapped one kid.

'He does,' insisted Jody. 'The police have arrested him for arson, and the judge is demanding he be tried as an adult. That means he could get as much as ten years.'

'Mark didn't tell us that,' said Roy, a look of worry finally crossing his face. 'We knew he got arrested, but I thought he got out on regular bail . . . no fuss.'

'There's plenty of fuss,' said Jody. 'Why would I lie? My mom defended Mark the last time he was in trouble.'

'Yeah,' mumbled Roy. 'And I hear she got him off.'

'Well, she's not sure she can do it this time,' said Jody. 'Look, we all want the same thing. To see Mark proved innocent. The best way to do that is to find the person who really started the fire.'

'Yeah, if I catch the creep, he won't have any knee-caps left.' Roy swung his hammer to demonstrate what he might do.

'He or she,' said Jody automatically. 'A girl could start a fire just as easily as a guy.'

'What a time to teach the Bullets a lesson in women's liberation,' whispered Jake.

'Shh,' said Jody.

'Why is that guy always whispering in your ear?' asked Roy suspiciously.

'Good question,' said Jody. 'He's my brother.'

'Look,' said Roy, 'we got a lot of work to do. We're trying to clean this place up again. We can't waste time talking to kids like you.'

'We'll help you,' said Jody.

Robie and Jake looked at each other.

'Why would you want to do that?' asked one of the gang, sounding very suspicious.

'Why not?' asked Jody. 'People are supposed to help each other out after a fire. Back in the frontier days whenever anyone had a fire, the whole town would help them rebuild. We're from the same town. Most of us even go to the same school.'

'That's the old frontier spirit,' said Jake, and this time Roy allowed himself a little smile.

'Your sister is quite a character, isn't she?' he said.

Jake smiled. 'You guessed it.'

'I don't like it,' said one of the kids in the gang. 'These kids aren't Bullets. I know them. They're all little teacher's pets.'

'Right,' said Jake. 'That must be why most of my teachers want to put me in the dog-house.'

'Or the nut-house,' added Jody.

'Look,' said Roy, 'as long as they're here, they can help. We need all the help we can get. Besides, just because they're helping us, it doesn't make them Bullets or anything.'

'What can we do to help?' asked Jody.

'We're just trying to clean up some of this mess,' said Roy. 'We were turning this house into three different modern apartments. It was all Mark's idea.'

9

THE ROOKIE

'Jody! Is that you?' demanded a voice.

Jody had plunged into the wreckage and was covered with black soot as she stuffed soggy plasterboard into rubbish bags. Jody looked up to see Mark standing in front of her.

'What are you doing here?' he demanded.

'Boy, I'm getting sick of being asked that question,' said Jody. 'I'm just helping out. Robie and Jake are around here somewhere.'

'I know,' said Mark. 'I saw them in the front room.' Mark gave the rubble a disgusted look. 'It's useless,' he said. 'We might as well just abandon this building . . . the way its real owners did. We'll never be able to renovate it now.'

'Who were the real owners?' asked Jody.

'I don't know,' said Mark, shrugging. 'This building was abandoned for the last couple of years. Nobody lived here but a couple of rats. Well, more than a couple. You should have seen the rat nests we found here when we started cleaning it up.'

'How did you get permission to renovate it?' Jody asked.

'You make it sound so clean-cut,' said Mark. 'It wasn't any great idea. At first we just started using it as a hideout for the gang. This whole block is full of burned-out houses. You've been to our apartment. We live in a housing project . . . crumbling walls, filthy, stinking hallways . . . tiny rooms built more like a prison than a home. And for that my dad has got to pay a lot of money every month, for nothing.' Mark sounded spiteful. 'I know we're supposed to be grateful to the city for giving us "low income housing", but it's not the same as owning your own home? My dad's out of work . . . *again*. He's drinking pretty heavy, *again*. But *I* want something that will be *ours*. Something that nobody can take away from me.'

Jody kept very quiet as Mark talked. He hadn't raised his voice, but he sounded so intense Jody felt as if he were shouting.

Suddenly Mark's attention was broken. He glanced up. Jody turned around. Mary Aurelio stood in the doorway, leaning against the door-jamb.

'You explaining the facts of life to the rookie?' said Mary.

'Leave her alone,' said Mark. 'At least she came to help clean up.'

'I'm sure she's a marvellous little helper,' said Mary, smiling at Jody in a patronising way. 'Fang and I already welcomed her.'

Jody felt both furious and embarrassed, and the two emotions played back and forth, leaving her unable to say anything.

'Get out of here,' insisted Mark. 'You thought fixing this place up was stupid. You started hanging around with the Razors. You're with them. You've made your choice.'

'This is a free country,' retorted Mary. 'I don't belong to anyone.'

Jody looked up at Mary with new respect and more than a little curiosity. Exactly where *did* Mary belong. If she had left the Bullets, why was she back hanging around. Was she a

43

Bullet or a Razor? Maybe it wasn't all over between Mark and Mary.

Jody couldn't decide whether she should leave the room or not. Clearly something was going on between Mary and Mark that was very personal, yet Jody decided to stay. She justified it to herself that she was only being a good investigator, but she knew that she didn't trust Mary, and if she were honest with herself, which Jody usually was, she knew she was slightly jealous.

Mary gave Jody a dirty glance as if saying, 'Get lost, kid,' but Jody busied herself in the corner, gathering bits and pieces of debris and putting them into her big green rubbish bag.

Mary seemed to realise Jody wasn't going to budge, so she decided to ignore her. 'Why did the pigs arrest *you*?' she asked.

'You know about my past record,' said Mark. 'And besides, they got enough evidence to lock me up for a long time. They found my fingerprints on a paraffin can in the back yard . . . and that paraffin can was *empty*.'

Mary stole another glance at Jody. She moved up closer to Mark, but Jody could still hear her. 'You didn't do it, did you?' she whispered. 'Did somebody pay you to burn this place down?'

Mark shoved her away from him so hard that she stumbled and fell into the rubbish piled in the corner. 'You think I could be bought just like that?' he said, snapping his fingers. For a second Jody was worried Mark was going to strike Mary, but then he got control of himself. 'You decided you didn't want to be a Bullet,' he said. 'Stick to your decision. Go back to the Razors.' Then, without looking back at Jody, he left the room.

'Are you all right?' Jody asked Mary.

Mary picked herself up. 'I don't need your help,' she said.

She was now as covered with soot from the fire as Jody. Mary tried to dust herself off. 'What are you staring at?' she said accusingly to Jody.

'Nothing,' said Jody. 'I wasn't staring. I'm sorry.'

'What are you sorry about?' asked Mary. 'I don't need that creep Mark. Let him get out of his own mess.' Mary sounded tough, but Jody could hear in her voice that she was hurt.

'Why did you call me a rookie?' asked Jody.

''Cause that's what you are,' said Mary. 'Hanging around here, like you belong. Well, you don't. You're just a rookie. You haven't proved yourself.'

'What do you have to do to prove yourself around here?' asked Jody.

Mary laughed, almost nastily. 'Things you haven't even dreamed of over there in your nice house, or in school with your good grades. We got initiation rites that will have you running home to your mamma like the little girl that you are.'

Jody straightened up. She was at least three inches taller than Mary in stocking feet. But Mary was wearing wedgie sandals with three-inch soles and an even higher heel. Jody, as usual, was wearing sneakers.

'I don't understand,' said Jody. 'Are you a Bullet or a Razor? You can't be both.'

Mary took off one of her sandals and rubbed her foot. She seemed to have twisted her ankle when Mark pushed her.

'It's none of your business,' she said, hopping up and down on one foot.

'People are telling me that an awful lot lately,' said Jody.

'Well you'd better start listening,' warned Mary, 'or you're gonna be in big trouble. You're nothing but the lowest rookie. You want to play here, you got to make a reputation. You put in your time. You can't just waltz in and expect everyone to stand to attention . . . because your good grades don't count for nothing here!'

10

A LIST OF SUSPECTS

'I'm sticking to the track team,' said Robie with a sigh as they got on their bicycles at the end of the day.

'Why?' asked Jody.

'Because,' snapped Robie, 'I've never worked so hard, and the harder I worked the meaner all the Bullets were to me. They kept calling me "rookie" and teasing me. Who needs it?'

'I'm sorry,' said Jody. 'I got you into it.'

'Well, it certainly wasn't that old frontier spirit you talked about,' said Robie. 'You know, one for all and all for one. They acted like I was trespassing.'

'I got the feeling the real frontier was a lot more like that than we know,' said Jake. 'Probably whenever the settlers helped each other after a fire, they were really trying to keep an eye on their neighbours because they thought one of them might have started the fire.'

'I admit the Bullets weren't very gracious,' said Jody.

Jake laughed. 'That's certainly one way of putting it. I kept being called "hey punk". Nobody even bothered to find out my name.'

'Well, they're suspicious,' said Jody. 'Wouldn't you be? They live in the slums and they know we don't. They were trying to fix the place up, and then suddenly all their work went up in smoke. It's easy for us. We have a nice place to live, and we know if the worst happened and our house did burn down, Mom has insurance and she earns good money. We'd have another nice home soon enough, but it's not the same for Mark and the Bullets.'

'I guess you're right,' said Robie. 'Still, they could have been a little nicer. Why do they call us rookies?'

'Apparently any new kids like us are called rookies – at least until we prove ourselves. That's what Mary seemed to be telling me,' said Jody.

'Yeah, well, I think I've got better things to do than try to prove myself to the Bullets,' said Robie. 'I'd better go. I've got to get home for dinner.'

'We'd better ride out of the neighbourhood with you,' said Jake. 'You don't want to tangle with Fang again. I'm glad she left him at home. What was she doing there anyhow? I thought she was a Razor.'

'I don't know,' said Jody. 'I think she's not too happy with her choice.'

'Bullets, Razors . . . these folks sure do go in for friendly names.'

Jody laughed uneasily. She felt badly about getting her best friend messed up in the troubles of Northtown. Once they passed Vickers Stadium Robie left them.

Jody and Jake biked the rest of the way home in silence. When they got there, their mother was already home from the office.

'You two look as if you've been making mud pies,' said Mrs Markson, taking in their soot-covered clothes. 'Where have you been?' she asked.

'In Northtown,' said Jake. 'We're trying out for rookie of the year.'

'What exactly does that mean?' asked Mrs Markson. 'And

47

what were the two of you doing in Northtown. Were you with Mark?'

'Bull's-eye,' said Jake. 'Jody is on one of her crusades.'

Mrs Markson looked at Jody with concern. Jody, who normally was so neat and clean and determined-looking, seemed dishevelled and dejected. She didn't even rise to her brother's bait.

'Why don't you take your shower first?' said Mrs Markson. 'I thought we'd go out for Chinese food tonight.'

'Okay,' said Jake. 'I'm too tired to cook anyhow. Being a teenage gang member ain't all it's cracked up to be. I thought it would mean hanging around looking tough. Instead I spent the whole day putting soggy plasterboard into rubbish bags. I ask you, would anyone want to make a movie called "I Was a Teenage Dustman"?'

'Oh, go soak your head,' said Jody.

'Gladly,' answered Jake, and he went upstairs.

Jody looked down at her filthy clothes. 'I'd better not sit down anywhere,' she said quietly. 'I'll leave big black marks. I'll go up to my room and change and wait for Jake to finish his shower.'

'Come into the kitchen,' said Mrs Markson. 'Let's have some lemonade.'

'I'm tired, Mom,' said Jody warningly.

'I know,' said Mrs Markson, 'but we have to talk. I don't like your going to Northtown without telling me.'

Jody played with her long brown hair, twirling it slightly around her finger. It was one of her few nervous habits.

Mrs Markson smiled at her daughter. 'Come on, honey,' she said. 'You've got to tell me what you've been up to.'

Jody nodded. She followed her mother into the kitchen. Mrs Markson poured them both a big glass of lemonade. She moved Jody's glass across the kitchen counter. 'Okay, partner, drink up,' she said.

Jody smiled and sipped her lemonade. 'There,' said her mother. 'At least you smiled. You looked so glum that I wasn't sure I could get a smile out of you.'

'It's just that it's so depressing in Northtown,' said Jody. 'And everything seems so mixed up with Mark.'

'Not everything,' corrected Mrs Markson. '*You* seemed mixed up about Mark. When he ran out on us last night I was furious. Arson is a terrible crime, and I didn't know if I wanted to defend an arsonist. I've been doing some research. Arson fires killed more than a thousand people in 1979 and destroyed more than three billion dollars worth of property. One thousand people, Jody. The courts are under a lot of pressure to crack down on arsonists.'

Mrs Markson sighed. 'In some ways, arson is the most vile of all crimes. Sometimes when I defend a murderer I can honestly understand why someone would kill in passion or fear. I think we all have murderous passions that we have to learn to control. I remember when you and Jake were little, I would always hear you or Jake scream, "I'll kill you!", but you learned to love each other and to control your rage. But some people can't, and I can understand, or at least sympathise with that. However, to start a fire, and not care whom you hurt or kill . . . I can't think of a worse crime.'

'I agree,' said Jody softly.

'I didn't mean to lecture you,' said Mrs Markson. 'I've just been so upset about this case. Mark called me this morning. He gave me a rather lame excuse about why he ran off last night. I've had my researcher do some work on Mark's case. It doesn't look good.'

'I know,' said Jody. 'The fingerprints on the paraffin can.'

'Yes,' said Mrs Markson, 'but there were other things. Mark hasn't been a little angel. I guess you don't get to be gang leader of something called the Bullets for nothing. There have been quite a few arrests for criminal trespassing,

49

and a few other incidents. The Bullets were once caught in a gang war with the Razors, and two kids were knifed. They were all right, thank goodness.'

'But Mark wasn't found guilty of knifing them,' protested Jody.

'No,' said Mrs Markson. 'According to rumours he wanted to stop the fight, but once it started he was definitely in the middle of it.'

'In short,' said Jody, 'you're trying to tell me that you think Mark might be guilty.'

'I don't know what to think,' said Mrs Markson. 'I'm only telling you that I think this is going to be a very messy trial, and I think you should stay out of it.'

'That's what Mark seems to think, too,' said Jody.

'Well,' said Mrs Markson, 'that's the first time he seems to be showing any sense.'

'But Mother,' protested Jody, 'you've let me help on other cases, and this time you really *need* me. The Bullets aren't much on talking to outsiders, even other teenagers, much less adults. Jake and I have a much better chance of finding out who else might have started the fire than you would.'

Mrs Markson ran her hands through her short curly hair. 'You're right,' admitted Mrs Markson. 'I interviewed one of the Bullets, David Ruggerio. He was one of the prime witnesses at the fire. He was the one who was almost injured. He was the last one out of the building.'

'I remember,' said Jody. 'I saw a fire fighter bring him out.'

'Well, Ruggerio could not seem to get it through his head that I was there to help Mark. He kept repeating, "I've got nothing to say, and you can't make me. I know my rights!" I told him that his rights didn't have anything to do with speaking to his friend's lawyer, but he didn't seem to under-stand.'

'I know David,' said Jody. 'At least a little. Most of these kids go to school with us. They just hang out with a completely different crowd. But I think if I can get them to trust me, I could find out a lot. I've already begun to find out things that might help you.'

Mrs Markson looked doubtful. 'I don't want to put you and Jake in danger,' she said.

'Come on, Mom,' objected Jody. 'You know we can take care of ourselves.'

Mrs Markson laughed. 'You're right, honey,' she said. 'You have certainly proved that time and again.'

'And you have to admit that we have a much better chance of getting closer to Mark's friends than you do,' said Jody.

'Right again,' admitted Mrs Markson. 'Only, I want you and Jake to report to me everything that is going on. No keeping anything to yourself this time.'

Jody looked down at the floor. She knew her mother was referring to the times she had waited until the last minute to catch the culprit.

'I agree,' said Jody.

'Well, what have you learned so far?' asked Mrs Markson.

'I've gathered quite a list of suspects,' said Jody. 'I don't have any evidence, but I've found plenty of people who might have a reason to frame Mark.'

Mrs Markson suddenly looked very interested. She took out a pen and paper. 'Shoot,' she said.

'Well, first of all, there is Joey Hennessey. He's the leader of the rival gang. He makes fun of Mark's plan to rehabilitate abandoned buildings, but I've heard that several members of the Razors are jealous that the Bullets are learning real skills that could get them jobs.'

'Joey Hennessey,' Mrs Markson repeated.

'Then there is Mary Aurelio,' said Jody. 'She used to be Mark's girl friend. They broke up about a month ago. She also thought Mark was a sissy for working on the building, and according to rumours, she is supposedly going out with Joey now. But I met her and I don't think she knows what she wants. Finally, there's Roy Washington,' said Jody. 'He's Mark's second-in-command, but I heard some rumours that some of the Bullets think that Roy wants to push Mark out and take over the gang for himself.'

Mrs Markson tapped her pen on the kitchen table thoughtfully. She looked at her list.

- Joey Hennessey
- Mary Aurelio
- Roy Washington

'I'll have my investigators see if they can turn up something on one of them,' she said.

'Great,' said Jody. 'Only . . . I keep feeling that there is something, or someone, that we have definitely missed . . . some motive that we haven't even thought of yet.'

11

JAKE MAKES A KILLING

'Do you want to go to the swap meet with me?' asked Mrs Markson the next Saturday morning. Every Saturday, one of Mrs Markson's best friends, Kendra Ferguson, ran an outdoor swap meet in the parking lot at Vickers Stadium.

'Are you getting rid of any junk?' asked Jody, who hated the fact that both Jake and Mrs Markson were always picking up things at the swap meet that they never used.

'Well . . .' admitted Mrs Markson. 'I haven't got around to cleaning out the garage, but I thought I'd just go and poke around.'

'Let's go,' said Jake.

'Okay,' said Jody. 'But I think I'll take my bike. I might not want to stay very long.'

Jody and Jake both took their bikes, and they met Mrs Markson there. By eleven in the morning, the lot was already full of people setting up their card tables with every conceivable thing to sell, from broken china to odd pieces of machinery.

Jake started looking around eagerly. 'Hey, Jody, look at this!' he shouted, holding up an old tin can that apparently once had held paint. It looked as if it was from the 1920s. It

53

had a very stylish art deco design printed in black and white.

'Isn't that terrific?' said Jake. 'It's only one dollar.'

'It's an empty paint can,' said Jody. 'What good is it?'

'What good is it . . .?' stammered Jake indignantly. 'Why, it's beautiful . . . it's –'

'It'll wind up in the garage with all the other junk you buy at these swap meets.'

'It's a perfect can for putting junk in,' said Jake, and he reached in his pocket, pulled out a dollar and gave it to the woman selling it. She smiled happily, obviously thinking she had got a good price for something she would have just thrown out anyway.

Jody and Jake walked through the crowded swap meet, Jake happily swinging his new purchase.

Suddenly a hand reached out and grabbed Jake, twirling him around.

'Where did you get that can?' the man demanded.

Jake stared at him. 'At one of the tables,' said Jake. 'Let go of my arm, mister.'

The man dropped Jake's arm. Jake rubbed his forearm. The man had an iron grip.

'I'm sorry,' said the man. He seemed to try to smile. 'Is that can for sale?'

'Nope,' said Jake. 'I just bought it. It's mine.'

'I'll buy it from you,' said the man.

'No, thanks,' said Jake. He started to leave with Jody. The man grabbed his arm again. Jake looked down at the muscular hand gripping his wrist.

'I'll give you ten dollars for it,' said the man.

Jake looked at the guy as if he thought he was a little crazy. 'Thanks, but no thanks,' said Jake. 'I really like it.'

Jody stared at her brother. She couldn't believe he didn't want to make an easy nine dollars.

'Twenty,' said the man.

Now it was Jake's turn to stare. He couldn't believe his ears. Before Jake could answer, the man raised his offer to thirty-five. Jake was so shocked that he couldn't answer.

'Fifty!' said the man. 'But that's my final offer.'

'Sold,' croaked Jake. He had refused to sell in the beginning only because he hadn't liked the man. He really wasn't that much in love with the old paint can.

The man grinned. 'I'll have to write you a cheque,' he said. 'I don't have enough cash. You drive a hard bargain.' The man whipped out his cheque-book. 'Whom shall I make it out to?' he asked.

Jake seemed so surprised he could still hardly talk.

'Jake Markson,' said Jody.

The man finished writing the cheque and handed it to Jake. 'Thanks again, kid. If you've got any other tin cans in your collection, I'd be glad to see them.'

'Uh . . . great!' stammered Jake. The man walked away, happily carrying Jake's paint can.

'FIFTY DOLLARS!' screamed Jake. 'I JUST MADE FIFTY DOLLARS!'

'Forty-nine,' corrected Jody. 'Remember you paid a dollar.'

Jake was so excited he could hardly see straight. He waved the cheque in front of Jody. 'Do you believe it?'

'No,' said Jody, looking at the name on the cheque. 'John Walker . . . well, you meet some crazy collectors around here.'

'Hey!' said Jake. 'What if that was a really rare can and it was worth more?'

'Don't get greedy,' warned Jody. 'Hey . . . Walker. That reminds me . . . wasn't that the name of the fireman who Mom said helped Mark.'

'Your ability to remember names never ceases to amaze

me,' said Jake. 'But I'm sure that's not the same Walker. Somehow I can't imagine a fireman spending fifty dollars on an old paint can.'

'An *empty* paint can,' added Jody. 'You're right. I know they don't make much money. Anyhow . . . the fire station for Northtown is right around here. Let's go see if we can find him.'

'You're asking *me* if I want to go to a fire station?' said Jake. 'Does a dog want a steak bone? Let's move it.'

The fire station for Northtown was directly behind Vickers Stadium. There was a five-by-five cubicle at the front of the fire station. Inside the small partitioned area there was a man writing in a journal.

'Can you tell me where to find Fireman Walker?' Jody asked.

'Sure. He's in the back.' The man turned and talked into an intercom. 'Ben, there are some kids here who want to talk to you.'

A few seconds later, Ben Walker came out and greeted them with a smile. Jody recognised him as the same man who had been hit by a piece of wood at the fire.

'Hi,' he said, 'can I help you?'

'We have a few questions,' said Jody.

Ben Walker smiled. He was a tall man, not fat, but heavily built. His wrists were big and knobby. He had a wide face and sandy-coloured hair. Most of all, he looked strong.

'Are you doing a paper for school?' he asked.

'Not exactly,' said Jody. 'We wanted to ask you about the fire in Northtown.'

'Which fire in Northtown?' asked Fireman Walker. 'We get about five a day, at least.'

Before Jody could answer, bells suddenly started to ring. Fireman Walker held up his hand indicating to Jody and

56

Jake to keep quiet, and he listened. Two short rings, pause, five rings, and then three.

'Two-five-three, McPherson and Kendall,' said Ben Walker. 'Each signal tells us which box was pulled.' The fire fighters rushed out from a room behind the apparatus and jumped onto the engine, grabbing their heavy rubber coats as they went.

'Step out of the way, kids,' said Ben Walker. 'If you want to wait, we may be back right away. Or it may be a while.'

He walked out into the middle of the street and stopped traffic, while another fire fighter eased the big engine out of the fire station.

Jody held her ears as the siren went off right next to her. Within seconds the fire station was empty. The doors closed, a sign on the door telling them 'anyone reporting a fire should call in on the box at the corner'.

'Now what?' asked Jake. 'Maybe we should follow them. Let's go to McPherson and Kendall.'

'We're going to stay right here and wait,' said Jody. 'I chased one fire with you and that was one too many.'

'But they might be gone a long time fighting the fire,' protested Jake. 'And it might be a spectacular fire.'

'No dice,' said Jody. 'We're staying here, or at least *I'm* staying here. *You* go chase them if you want.'

'I want,' said Jake, getting on his bike.

12

ARSON IS A COWARD'S CRIME

Jody watched him go. She locked her bike to a NO PARKING sign. She had barely got the chain around the lock when she looked up and saw the fire engine rounding the corner.

The fire fighters jumped off the engine and helped the driver guide the big machine back into the fire station. 'Come on, Sterns,' shouted one of the fire fighters. 'Time to get your great Irish stew.'

'Hold it, Mazelli,' shouted the other man good-naturedly. 'You can't hurry a great chef.'

'Yeah, but we might not have much time before the next alarm comes in. Get moving.'

Fireman Walker took off his heavy rubber coat. He seemed surprised to see Jody. 'Oh, hi. You're still here,' he said.

'You weren't gone very long,' said Jody.

'False alarm,' said Fireman Walker. 'If we could find the kid who did it, I'd throw him in jail.'

'I didn't know sending in a false alarm was a crime,' said Jody.

Ben Walker laughed bitterly. 'Yeah. Kids like you think it's a great thrill to pull that lever and watch all the excitement. It makes you feel big, doesn't it, to know you can be responsible for all the noise, the sirens, the air horns, and make all those big men stop their work and come just because you called.'

'Hey, wait a minute,' protested Jody. 'I never called in a false alarm in my life.'

Walker did a double take. 'Maybe,' he said. 'But after ten years on the job I'd like to see every person who pulls a false alarm locked up. We go on countless false alarms. And every time we go out for a false alarm somewhere, a fire could break out somewhere else, and we wouldn't be able to get there in time. I can remember many fires when if we hadn't been called on a false alarm we would have saved someone's life.'

'Hey, Ben,' said the fire fighter standing next to him, 'take it easy on the kid. She's right, you know. You can't lump all kids together.'

'I hate it when adults do that,' said Jody. 'But Mr Walker's right. I never really thought about false alarms before. And I do know kids at school who get a kick out of calling one. They sort of do it on a dare.'

'Call me Ben,' said Fireman Walker, smiling. 'Maybe you can do that school project on false alarms,' he said.

'But I didn't come here to talk to you about a school project,' said Jody. 'I came to talk to you about arson.'

Ben looked at Jody with new interest. 'Arson,' said Ben. 'Maybe we had better have a talk. Why don't you come in the back with me.'

'Okay,' said Jody. 'Only, my brother is around somewhere. He raced after you. He loves to watch fires. He must be biking back here.'

Ben took Jody firmly by the arm and guided her to the back of the fire station. Jody turned around to take one last look for Jake. Fireman Walker gripped her arm even tighter. As Jody walked by the pumpers and the ladders she stared at the neatly stacked hoses, folded in on each other like politely placed snakes. A fireman was hosing down the floor under the equipment.

'My brother is going to love this,' said Jody.

'I bet,' said Ben. Something in his voice made Jody look up. His face had turned grim again, as if he didn't trust her. Jody noticed again how firmly he had hold of her arm. She tried to shake it free. He gripped her even tighter.

'Let go, please,' Jody commanded politely.

'Just come with me,' insisted Fireman Walker.

'I will,' said Jody, 'as soon as you let go of my arm.'

Fireman Walker looked at her suspiciously. He loosened his hold on her arm, but rested his hand lightly on her elbow. He released it only when they reached the back of the fire station.

Jody was surprised to see a full kitchen, a sink, a stove and a refrigerator. A couple of men were playing cards and several were gathered around the end of the long room watching television. At the stove one of the men seemed to be preparing stew. He had red meat cut in cubes and he was browning the onions, sending up a delicious smell through the room.

Fireman Walker closed the door behind him and finally released Jody's arm. He indicated that Jody should sit at a table at the far end of the room from the television set. He sat down opposite Jody.

'Now,' he said sternly, 'exactly what do you want to tell me about the arson the other day.'

'You think I've come to confess,' said Jody in an astonished voice.

Fireman Walker shifted uneasily in his seat. He leaned forward eagerly. 'I think you'll feel a lot better once you've got it off your chest,' he said.

'But I didn't start it,' said Jody. 'What gave you that idea?'

'Don't be frightened,' said Fireman Walker. 'We can help you. I remember seeing you at the fire. If you have any information, it'll be easier for you if you tell us about it now.'

'Wait a minute,' said Jody. 'My mom is Mark's lawyer. I came to ask you some questions, but I certainly didn't come to confess.'

Fireman Walker hunched his shoulders up. He looked depressed. 'I'm sorry,' he said with a sigh. 'I guess I owe you an apology. I've been so anxious about that fire. Mark is a special person to me. It broke my heart when the fire master called me over and told me they had got an anonymous tip. Then when they told me about the fingerprints . . .' Ben's voice trailed off.

'Hey, Ben,' shouted one of the firemen, 'is there a Jody Markson in here?'

'That's me,' said Jody.

'Her brother is here, crawling all over our equipment,' said one of the firemen.

'That sounds like Jake,' said Jody.

Jake came into the back of the fire station. 'Hey, this is neat,' he said. 'I didn't realise you had kitchens back here.'

'On our salaries, we have to cook our own meals,' said the fireman. 'We take turns.'

'Now Jake will be a fire fighter for sure,' said Jody.

Fireman Walker smiled at Jake and seemed to loosen up for the first time. 'Do you want to be a fireman?' he asked.

Jake nodded his head yes.

'That's good to hear,' said the fireman. 'We don't hear of as many kids saying they want to be fire fighters any more. It's a good job. It's tough. It's the most dangerous job in America. Almost twice as many fire fighters get killed in the line of duty as police. It's not glamorous either. Anyone who has to crawl along a tenement corridor filled with smoke at three o'clock on a freezing morning knows it's not glamorous.'

'But you are real heroes,' said Jake. 'You do the work that nobody else will do.'

'Don't go becoming a fire fighter 'cause you want to be a hero,' warned the fireman. 'It's not that kind of job. You just do what you have to do. And it's a dirty job, especially today. It's one thing to have to risk your life to put out fires that started accidentally. It's another to lose your life because somebody figured out a way to make a fast buck.'

'How do people make money out of a fire?' asked Jody.

Fireman Walker laughed bitterly. 'Let me count the ways,' he said. 'The idea that vandals or street gangs like to start fires is mostly a myth. That's why I was so upset that they found Mark's fingerprints on that paraffin can. Most of the time someone makes money from arson. Someone collects insurance money. They buy a building cheap and they let it run down, cut off hot water, don't make repairs. Meanwhile, they go to an insurance company and they list the building as being worth a lot more than it is.' Fireman Walker shrugged his shoulders.

'But that couldn't be true in this case,' said Jody. 'The building wasn't owned by anybody.'

'It had been abandoned,' said Fireman Walker. 'But it was still owned on paper by something called "Bushmaster Enterprises." But nobody could find them. I started the paperwork to have the ownership transferred to Mark, but the city's machinery moves very slowly. The Buildings Department is always a mess. Somehow they lost my set of papers. I was trying to get it straightened out when the place burned down.'

'But Mark still wouldn't have reason to burn the building down. Somebody else had to have done it,' protested Jody.

Ben Walker just shook his head sadly. 'I told you. I

believed in Mark, but he's a kid who's been under a lot of pressure all his life. Maybe he just wasn't as strong as I thought he was. Arson is a coward's crime. You don't ever have to see your victim.'

Jody thought about Ben Walker's words. Somehow she knew Mark wasn't a coward.

Fireman Walker seemed to know what Jody was thinking. 'I don't think Mark's a coward either,' he said. 'He took a lot of kidding from his gang and friends when he started fixing the place up.'

'I know,' said Jody. 'The Razors call the Bullets sissies for learning carpentry.'

'Well, the Bullets weren't so willing when Mark first told them what he wanted to do. Luckily, my brother's in the construction business. I talked him into getting a crew together to teach the Bullets the building trade.'

'Your brother's name isn't John Walker, is it?' asked Jake.

Fireman Walker looked at him in astonishment. 'How did you know that?'

Jake grinned. 'Does he collect old tin cans?'

'Collect them?' said Fireman Walker. 'He's a fanatic. He's lucky he's very rich because he'll spend more on one tin can than I'd spend taking my wife and me out for the fanciest dinner in town.'

'Like fifty dollars,' said Jake.

'Exactly,' said Fireman Walker. Then Jake told him what had happened at the swap meet.

'Well, he does have some cans that are worth a hundred dollars,' said Fireman Walker. 'There's even been an article about his collection in a magazine for people who like to collect weird things.'

'A hundred dollars!' cried Jake, turning to Jody. 'I was robbed.'

'You were lucky!' said Jody.

63

13

A DATE FOR
A GANG FIGHT

'A cowardly crime.' Jody repeated the words to Mark. They
were working in the back room of the abandoned house on
the next day. Harpo had followed Jody and Jake from home,
and he had fallen asleep on a pile of wood shavings. Jody told
Mark of her visit to the fire station.

'Yeah, Ben told me about the papers being lost,' said
Mark. 'What a joke. He and I went down to the Buildings
Department to try to get it straightened out. They got all
these files lying around, piled up on desks. They give you this
incredible go-around. It'll probably turn out we don't own
this wreck after all.' Mark laughed bitterly.

Suddenly Harpo stood up, holding his legs and tail stiffly.

'Hey, Mark,' taunted a voice from the hallway. 'You still
giving the rookie your personal attention?'

Mary Aurelio walked into the room. Fang was beside her.
Fang also immediately stiffened and began to growl.

'Hey, careful,' said Mark. 'We don't want a dog-fight.'

'Mark! Mark!' cried a voice from outside. 'The Razors are
here!'

Mark looked at Mary suspiciously. 'Did *you* bring them?'
he asked.

Mary put on her most innocent expression. 'You're blaming me for almost everything lately. Maybe the Razors came to see what pretty work you do.'

Mark stalked out of the room, leaving Jody alone with Mary.

The two dogs were separated by a mere fifteen feet or so. Fang suddenly lay down like a crouching tiger, emitting a low growl.

'You'd better be careful about your dog,' warned Jody, watching Fang closely. Harpo walked up to Fang stiffly. Fang shot up to his full height. Harpo advanced with a dancing action of his forepaws. Harpo lowered his ears and kept his forehead perfectly flat.

'He's trying to get him to play,' said Jody.

'Fang won't play,' said Mary. She grabbed Fang roughly by the collar.

'Come on,' she said. 'I don't want to miss the fun.'

Mary dragged Fang out to the front porch. Jody followed her. A group of Razors had gathered around the porch. Joey Hennessey stood in front of his gang.

All of the Bullets had pushed onto the porch, and it sagged dangerously, having already been weakened by the fire. Roy stood in front of the Bullets. As Jody and Mary came out, Mark pushed his way through the gang and stood next to Roy.

'What do you want, Joey?' asked Mark.

'They want a fight,' answered Roy. 'And this time we're not backing away from them. They got no right to come around here. This here is Bullet territory.'

Before anyone could answer, Fang broke away from Mary's grip and bounded off the porch. Harpo followed.

'Hey! A dog-fight!' shouted Joey, as he and several Razors stepped out of the way of the two dogs.

Harpo's tail shot up and he walked stiffly up to Fang.

'They're testing each other,' said Jody.

'Don't you want to get them apart?' said Mark.

'Wait a second,' said Jody. 'Neither looks like he's going to attack.' Jody loved animals. She was a volunteer at the animal society, and she read every book she could find on animal behaviour. 'Watch their ears and the corners of their mouths,' continued Jody. 'Harpo is very sure of himself. Even though Fang's bigger, he won't back down, and as long as he won't back down, they probably won't fight.' Harpo offered his hind parts confidently to Fang. Fang sniffed. They circled each other warily.

'How old is Fang?' asked Jody.

'Just a year and a half,' said Mary. 'He's almost full grown.'

Joey Hennessey let out a long sigh of respect. 'He's still growing?' he said, looking in awe at Fang's size.

Finally Fang went over to the lamp-post and relieved himself on it. 'He's telling Harpo that he won't challenge him,' whispered Jody. 'He realised Harpo's older. Now they should play. Fang's younger, and he knows he owes Harpo some respect, and Harpo really doesn't like to fight unless he has to.'

Fang now came forward, stretching up his neck and raising his tail. The corners of his mouth had an upward tilt, and his jaws opened to reveal his tongue.

Jody breathed a sigh of relief.

Both gangs had been watching the dogs; now their attention went back to each other.

Mark turned to Joey threateningly. 'Get off our property,' he warned.

'Oh?' Joey laughed. 'Is this *your* property? I thought this property was condemned.' The gang behind Joey all laughed.

'Yeah,' said the boy standing next to Joey. 'They burned out all the cockroaches.'

'Very funny,' said Mark. 'Now, get off our lawn.'

Joey looked down at the debris lying all around the few square feet that made up the house's lawn. 'Aw . . . you don't want us punks dirtying up your pretty lawn,' he said.

'Get lost,' said Mark.

Joey turned to his gang. 'Uh-oh,' he said in a sarcastic voice. 'Did you hear that? The nasty boy threatened me.' Then his voice turned serious. 'Okay, Mark. Where do you want to meet and when?'

'You name the place,' said Mark. 'But no knives, no guns. Just you and me.'

'Wait a minute,' interrupted Jody. 'You're crazy, Mark. You're out on bail on a serious crime. You can't be fighting. The police will throw you back in jail so fast, you won't know what hit you.'

'Isn't that cute, Mark. Your gal defender is at it again.'

'Just shut up, Jody,' said Mark sharply. 'This has nothing to do with you.'

'But you're being stupid,' said Jody.

Mark shot Jody a dirty look. 'Name your time and place,' he repeated to the Razors.

'What about in the parking lot at Vickers Stadium, Saturday night at midnight?' answered Joey.

'Midnight,' whispered Jody.

'Is that past your bedtime?' whispered one of the Bullets standing next to her. Jody hadn't realised she had spoken out loud.

'Saturday midnight at Vickers Stadium,' said Mark. 'Perfect.'

Jody shook her head. The one thing she knew was that it was not perfect. She looked up the street at Harpo and Fang happily playing with each other. 'Why can't people be more like dogs?' she whispered to herself.

14

HUNTING FOR
MORE THAN A HOUSE

'You've got to be kidding!' exclaimed Jake when Jody told him what had happened. 'Mark has got himself involved in a gang fight!'

'We've got to stop them,' said Jody. 'Today is Tuesday. We have just four days.'

'Oh, right,' said Jake. 'We'll just walk right in and talk them out of it.'

'I already tried that,' said Jody. 'It didn't work.'

Jake looked at his sister and laughed out loud. 'I was kidding,' he said.

'Well, I did try to talk Mark out of it,' said Jody defensively. 'It's stupid.'

'That must have gone over big,' said Jake.

'What do you mean?' asked Jody.

'Calling him stupid,' said Jake.

'I didn't call *him* stupid. I told him what he was doing was *stupid*.'

'Well, I grew up with you,' said Jake, 'and I can *sometimes* understand how your ultra-logical mind works, but I can see how Mark might have got mad. After all, his grades aren't that terrific.'

'Mark is plenty smart,' said Jody. 'I don't think he would have become a leader of the Bullets or thought of the idea of rehabilitating that building if he wasn't very smart.'

'Okay, okay,' said Jake. 'But if he's so smart, how come he gets in so much trouble?'

Jody shrugged her shoulders.

'Come to think of it,' said Jake, 'you're the smartest person I know and you get in trouble all the time.'

'You are *not* helping,' complained Jody.

'I'm sorry,' said Jake seriously. 'But honestly, Jody, we're not exactly the most popular two kids in Northtown. I can't see us going there at midnight and stopping a gang fight. We could get ourselves killed.'

'All right, but what legitimate reason could we have for going to Vickers Stadium?' asked Jody.

'At midnight?' exclaimed Jake. 'I can just see us telling Mom we're going to Vickers Stadium at midnight.'

'Well, forget about midnight for a second,' said Jody. 'Hey! Wait a minute. What about the swap meets?'

'Great idea,' said Jake sarcastically. 'They always have them at midnight.'

'Well . . .' said Jody, 'there's always a first time. What's Kendra Ferguson's number?'

'It must be in Mom's book,' said Jake. 'But are you actually going to call her and suggest a midnight swap meet?'

'Do you have any better ideas?' said Jody.

Jody called her mother's friend, Kendra Ferguson.

'A swap meet at midnight?' repeated Kendra when she heard Jody's idea.

'I thought it would be a novelty,' said Jody. 'I bet lots of people might want to come.'

'You know,' said Kendra, 'it's not a bad idea. At least as a one-time thing. I'll call the stadium owners and see if I can get permission to use the parking lot. I'll call you back if it's on.'

'Great,' said Jody.

'By the way, does Jake have any more paint cans to sell? John Walker got a gem for his collection from Jake.'

'Don't tell Jake,' said Jody. 'He still thinks he could have got more money.'

'He got a huge profit,' said Kendra. 'Tell him not to get too greedy.'

'That's what I told him,' said Jody. She hung up. 'Kendra Ferguson says not to get too greedy,' she told Jake.

'What about the midnight swap meet?' asked Jake.

'She liked the idea,' said Jody.

A little while later, Kendra Ferguson called to say the swap meet was on. Jody told her that she would help put up posters announcing the event.

'It'll be great,' said Jody excitedly. 'The Bullets and the Razors will show up at the parking lot, and all these people will be there. They won't be able to fight.'

'Then what?' objected Jake. 'They would probably just pick another night. We can't keep following them around . . . the roving swap meet.'

'One night at a time,' said Jody. 'I have the feeling that everyone's temper is just hot because of the fire. If I can solve the mystery of who started the fire, Mark might not feel he *has* to fight.' Jody went to her desk and took out a blank piece of typing paper. She wrote:

BARGAINS! BARGAINS!
SPECIAL LATE-NIGHT
SWAP MEET
VICKERS STADIUM
Saturday, May 12
MIDNIGHT

'Now, we've got to get them copied and start putting them up around town.'

'Won't the Bullets and Razors see them?' asked Jake.

'I don't think they're the type to go to swap meets,' said Jody. 'But just in case, we won't put any up in Northtown.'

Jody had one hundred copies of her poster copied, and then she and Jake bicycled all around town, posting their notices. Many people came by to look as they were taping their posters onto lamp-posts.'

'Oh, a late-night swap meet,' said one man. 'It sounds like fun. I think maybe I have a few things in my garage I'd like to get rid of.'

'Bring them along,' said Jody. 'See you then.'

As they taped one of their last posters Jody suddenly shouted, 'Walker Construction and Real Estate!'

Jake shook his head as if his ears were ringing, and in truth Jody had shouted directly in his ear. 'Hum a few bars and I'll sing it,' he said.

'What?' said Jody.

'You just shouted in my ear and I was trying to make a joke.' said Jake.

'Walker Construction is the group that's been helping Mark. Remember . . . he's the guy who bought your can.'

'Right, maybe we can go in and ask to look at his can collection.'

'Let's go in,' she said decisively.

'It's the middle of business hours,' objected Jake. 'They're not going to want two kids interrupting their day and asking questions.'

'We are not "two kids",' said Jody. 'We are two potential customers. Come on.'

Jake followed Jody into the office. It was a sprawling one-storey building with wall-to-wall carpeting and several desks lined up behind each other. There was a partition dividing the public space from what looked like private offices in the back.

Jody went up to the receptionist. 'Excuse me,' she said politely, 'can you help me?'

The receptionist looked up. 'I don't know honey,' said said, 'it depends on what you want.'

'I wanted to talk to somebody about some houses,' said Jody.

The receptionist stared at her. 'You look a little young to be buying a house.'

'Oh no, it's not me. My father lives in New York, and he is thinking of moving back here, and he asked me to make some inquiries for him,' explained Jody.

'Oh,' said the receptionist, looking a little doubtful. 'If you'll take a seat, I'll see if one of our agents can see you.'

Jody and Jake took a seat, and Jody picked up an old issue of *Time* magazine, trying to look as if she went around to estate agencies all the time.

'Jody,' whispered Jake, 'Dad isn't thinking of moving back here, is he?'

'No,' whispered Jody, 'but they don't know that.'

'Mr Bush will see you now,' said the receptionist. 'You're in luck. He's one of Mr Walker's partners.'

Mr Bush was a very friendly man with a receding hairline, which he made up for by growing long, elegant-looking sideburns. He held out his hand and greeted Jody with all the respect that he might give to his best customer.

'How do you do?' he said. 'My receptionist tells me that you are interested in some property. You're a little younger than our usual customer.'

Jody smiled politely at Mr Bush's rather heavy attempt at humour. 'Actually, I'm making some inquiries for my father,' she said. 'He lives in New York, and he's thinking about moving back here.'

'I see,' said Mr Bush, although he looked perplexed. 'Where do you live now?' he asked. 'You don't live in New York.'

'No. We live on Sullivan Street with our mother,' said Jody. 'My parents are divorced.'

'Now I do see,' said Mr Bush smilingly. 'And your father would like something in your neighbourhood?'

'No,' said Jody quickly. 'He wanted to know about something more in the centre of town. He doesn't have too much money and he was thinking about Northtown.'

'Northtown!' exclaimed Mr Bush.

'Well, it *is* centrally located,' said Jody, 'and I understand some very nice homes can be bought quite cheaply and then fixed up.'

Mr Bush stroked his sideburns. Then he leaned forward, as if he were about to tell Jody and Jake a very intimate secret. 'Your father may be quite a smart man,' he whispered. 'With the petrol shortage, many people are beginning to have second thoughts about Northtown. Right now that area is a little rough, but a lot of families from the suburbs are thinking of moving back into the centre of the city, and Northtown could be just the place.'

'The place for what?' asked Jake.

'*The* place . . . the place to invest in right now,' said Mr Bush.

'I've heard though that there is a lot of arson in the area,' said Jody, as if having second thoughts.

Mr Bush frowned. 'Oh, I don't know if I'd call it arson. There have been some accidental fires, and sometimes the street gangs in the neighbourhood just get a little rambunctious. But it's nothing that won't be controlled, especially once the neighbourhood starts to change.'

'I see,' said Jody. 'So you don't think there's an arson ring.'

'What exactly do you mean by "an arson ring", young lady?' asked Mr Bush.

Jody tried to look confused. 'Oh, you know,' she stammered. 'You hear so many rumours. My daddy told me he had heard rumours that some landlords were making a lot of money from insurance in Northtown.'

Jake coughed loudly and then pretended to choke.

'Excuse my brother,' said Jody. 'He gets these coughing fits.'

'I haven't heard any rumours like that,' said Mr Bush.

'Oh good,' said Jody. 'Then I can tell my father that somebody had probably been just talking his ear off.' She laughed. 'Probably they wanted to buy up all the good properties in Northtown themselves.'

'Probably,' repeated Jake. Jody gave him a dirty look.

'Anyhow, Mr Bush, do you have any properties for sale in Northtown?'

Mr Bush got up from behind his desk. He was a tall man and he towered over Jody and Jake. 'I don't think we have anything available right now,' he said. 'But we are expecting something to open up soon. What did you say your name is?' he asked.

'I'm afraid I forgot to give you my name,' said Jody. 'It's Markson.'

'Markson,' repeated Mr Bush. Then he smiled and held out his hand to Jody. 'If you leave your phone number and address with our receptionist, we'll call you as soon as something comes up.'

'That will be terrific,' said Jody. 'I know my father is eager to buy something as soon as possible.'

'I'm sure,' said Mr Bush.

Jake coughed again.

15

A PIECE IS MISSING

'There's a piece missing,' complained Jody, holding up a jigsaw puzzle box. It was Thursday night, and Jody had finally convinced her mother to go through their basement looking for things to take to the swap meet. Mrs Markson had agreed to let them stay up past curfew and to go. In fact, she had decided it was a good opportunity to get rid of many things she had been planning on throwing out for a long time.

'Do you think anyone will want a broken basketball hoop?' asked Jake.

'It wouldn't be hard to fix up,' mused Mrs Markson. 'Maybe we shouldn't sell it.'

'Mom,' said Jody, 'that's how we wind up with all this junk.'

Mrs Markson was an admitted hoarder. She hated to throw out anything. Jake took after her. Jody, on the other hand, liked to clean out her bookshelves once a year and give to the library the books she thought she wouldn't want again. Jake hated to give away a book. He always thought that maybe, just maybe, he'd need it or want to look at it again.

'How about that old stationary bicycle?' asked Mrs Markson, getting on it and starting to pedal. 'Remember? I got that for one of my exercise programmes. I was going to watch television and lose weight all at the same time.'

Chico and Harpo chased each other over the piles of boxes, and suddenly a pile of boxes fell to the floor. A pile of Mrs Markson's papers flew all over the place.

'CHICO! HARPO!' shouted Mrs Markson. 'What a mess!'

'It wasn't really their fault, Mom,' said Jody. She began to pick up her mom's papers and help her put them back into the boxes.

'You know going through stuff is not my favourite activity,' said Mrs Markson. 'What were you saying about a piece missing? Were you talking about Mark's case or the puzzle?'

'I'm not sure what I meant,' said Jody. 'You know that Ben Walker arranged for Mark to get permission for his gang to work on the abandoned house, and then the plans got lost. There's something fishy, but I'm not quite sure what. I just feel a piece is missing.'

'I found the piece,' said Jake, who had been rummaging in the back of the basement. He came up with a piece of a puzzle. Then he looked at it again. 'Whoops, wrong puzzle,' he said. 'Anyhow, we have a couple of hundred old jigsaw puzzles in a box back there.'

'Great,' said Mrs Markson. 'I'm sure that will fetch a lot of money at the swap meet.'

'Ah yes,' said Jake, 'Jody's famous swap meet. I hear she's got some spectacular entertainment set up . . . the fight of the century.'

'Shut up, Jake,' said Jody crossly.

'What is that about?' asked Mrs Markson.

'Oh, just Jake being cute,' said Jody.

'I know,' said Mrs Markson, 'but that doesn't explain why you are being so touchy.'

'I'm not,' said Jody.

Mrs Markson looked at her daughter closely. 'You aren't trying to solve this case by yourself, are you?' she asked.

'No, Mom,' said Jody. 'I've told you everything I know, but I'm not much further along than I was the first week. Mary Aurelio is still a mystery. She tried to break up with Mark because she thought his plan to fix up the house wasn't macho or something, but I can tell she really likes him. She still hangs out with the Bullets. She says she doesn't belong to anybody. I've got to admire her for saying that.'

'People can care for someone very much and still work to destroy them,' said Mrs Markson softly. 'Love and hate are very close, even among teenagers.'

'I know,' said Jody, 'but I have no proof against Mary either way. I am just getting a gut feeling she's innocent.'

'What about the other two suspects?' said Mrs Markson. 'Roy Washington, Mark's second-in-command. I interviewed him for the trial, and he was very unco-operative.'

'Roy is definitely jealous of Mark,' said Jake. 'I can vouch for that. When we were working together at the house, he just made one dig at Mark after another.'

'But when he's around Mark he never makes cracks,' said Jody. 'He lets Mark make the decisions.'

'I know,' said Jake, 'but I don't think he likes them. He was complaining how the Bullets were losing their reputation, and how everyone was making fun of them.'

'Not everybody,' corrected Jody. 'Just the Razors. As far as I can tell Joey Hennessey keeps needling the Bullets, and I think he's just jealous because he didn't think up the idea of rehabilitating a house by himself. All the Bullets are learning a trade and at least have a chance of getting a job, but the Razors have nothing, and they're turning into nothings.'

'That's a pretty harsh judgment, Jody,' said Mrs Markson.

'I know, Mom. But the Razors do nothing except make fun of Mark.'

'I believe you,' said Mrs Markson, 'but that doesn't make them arsonists. We keep forgetting the main point. Mark's fingerprints were found on the paraffin can, and nobody else's prints were. Unless I can somehow explain to the jury how his fingerprints got on that paraffin can, Mark is in big trouble, and we can make our list of other suspects as long as my arm, but it won't help.'

'Has the trial been scheduled yet?' asked Jody.

'It's on the docket, and we should start picking the jury next Monday,' said Mrs Markson.

Jody looked distraught, and Mrs Markson pitied her. 'Jody, we can't win every case,' she warned. 'You know that I'll do my best, but every lawyer loses sometimes.'

'Yes,' said Jody, 'but it's Mark who's going to have to go to jail if you lose.'

'I know,' said Mrs Markson. 'The worst thing about being a lawyer is feeling that you always could have done something more to keep your client out of jail, but sometimes you can't.'

'But you're talking as if you have lost already!' protested Jody.

Mrs Markson squared her shoulders. 'I certainly have *not*!' she objected. 'I'm going to fight my hardest and my best for Mark. I haven't given up . . . not by a long shot.'

'Yeah,' said Jake, 'but a long shot is what we're going to need if you're going to be able to explain away those fingerprints.'

'There's got to be something we've missed,' said Jody. 'I'm sure of it.'

16

WHAT'S GREEN AND DANGEROUS?

'You're coming to the swap meet, aren't you?' asked Jody. Robie was dressed in her track suit, having just finished her training.

'Yeah,' said Robie, 'but I still don't understand why you're having it at midnight. I'm supposed to run in a six-mile road race on Sunday and I'll be beat.'

'That's okay,' said Jake. 'I read somewhere that most runners think it's more important to get a good night's rest *two* nights before the race rather than the day before.'

'Okay, I'll try to get a good night's sleep tonight,' said Robie cheerfully. 'What are you guys doing right now? Want to come over to my house and sing me some lullabyes?'

'It's only four o'clock in the afternoon,' said Jody.

'Can't start getting that good night's sleep too early. Besides, I was only kidding about singing lullabyes. We can listen to some music. I've got some great new albums.'

'No, I have to go back to Northtown,' said Jody. 'They're going to be doing some painting today. Mark and the gang have torn down all the burned walls and rebuilt the new ones in the back room. I said that I would help.'

'And we're running a little short on time,' said Jake.

'What about your running?' asked Robie. Jake was a long-distance runner. He ran the two-mile in high school track meets, and he often ran the longer open road race. 'Haven't you entered the race on Sunday?'

'No,' answered Jake. 'I've been so busy being a "rookie Bullet" I haven't had much time to train.'

'You haven't really joined the Bullets?' asked Robie.

'No,' said Jody impatiently.

'But you have been spending almost every afternoon over at their house,' Robie pointed out. 'Some of the kids are beginning to talk about it. They said the Markson's are trying to prove something, but nobody knows what.'

'Well, they're right,' said Jody. 'I'm trying to prove Mark's innocent.'

'I don't think that's exactly what the gossipers had in mind,' said Jake.

'We can't let a bunch of gossip worry us,' said Jody. 'I'd better go.'

'If you can wait a minute while I change, I'll go with you,' said Robie.

Jody smiled at her friend. 'You don't have to,' she said. 'Once is enough.'

'How come you don't tell *me* that,' complained Jake good-naturedly.

'No, I want to come,' said Robie. 'To tell you the truth, I sort of like some of the kids in the Bullets. I was always scared of them before. They look so tough with their ripped jackets. I always thought they would bite my head off as soon as talk to me. But when I was working with them, even though they kept teasing me about being a rookie, some of them were kind of sweet and shy.'

'I know,' said Jody. 'I think they just put on that tough act for a show.'

'I don't think it's all an act,' warned Jake.

'Anyhow,' said Robie, 'wait for me a minute and I'll come with you. Only, let's bike a different route so we don't have to run into Fang again.'

'Good idea,' agreed Jody.

When they arrived at the house on Thornton Street Robie and Jake locked their bikes to a tree, and Jody wound her heavy chain around a NO PARKING sign.

'Here they come again,' said Roy from the porch. 'The Three Musketeers. You guys just don't give up.'

'Nope,' said Jake. 'You're just so much fun to be with we can't resist coming. How's the work going?'

Roy gave Jake a half-smile. 'Actually it's looking terrific. Somehow the fire got us going twice as fast. Some of the men from Walker Construction are here today. They're teaching us how to put in the wiring in the front rooms.'

'We're going to do some painting in the back,' said Jody. 'But can I meet the electrician?'

'Sure,' said Roy. 'Just don't get in his way.'

The front room was crowded with Bullets gathered around a tall thin man with balding hair and a moustache. He had a serious expression on his face. Mark stood next to him, listening intently.

'Wiring sounds much more scary than it is,' said the man. 'Modern wires and wiring devices make it easy and safe. Everything is made to work together. No electrical wiring must become exposed at any point where it could cause a shock, a short circuit or a fire. You guys have already had your fire, so you don't need to go through that again.

'All splices and joints in electrical wiring must be made inside what we call "boxes". The wiring goes inside the walls, but you have to be able to get at the boxes, so the boxes must be placed where the wiring can be permanently accessible. All wire runs must be continuous from box to box. No splices may be made outside the box.'

'How do you keep yourself from being electrocuted?' asked one boy.

'All your wire is grounded. I'll teach you about safety, but you don't work with live wires. Now, there are too many of you here for me to work with. I'd rather work with a small group of about three, and I'll teach them the specifics. They can be your electricians. If more of you are interested in becoming an electrician, we can work something out.'

'He seems like a nice man,' said Jody.

'Okay,' said Mark, 'who wants to work on the electricity?'

'I do!' shouted one kid.

'Yeah, you're a real hot wire,' said another.

'Maybe we should see if Mary wants to become an electrician,' joked one boy. 'She's a hot wire!'

Mark gave him a dirty look.

'Hey, how about the Markson girl. She's one of those women libbers.'

'Women liberationists,' corrected Jody.

'Excuuuse me!' said Roy, imitating Steve Martin.

'Anyhow, I wouldn't mind learning about wiring,' said Jody. The tall bald man scowled, and Jody couldn't tell whether he just didn't like the idea of teaching girls or whether he was getting tired of all the kidding around.

'All right,' said Mark. 'Jody, Roy and Al will work with Mr Benson.'

'Hey, Jody isn't really a Bullet,' complained one kid. 'She doesn't need a job. She's going to be a college girl.'

'At least,' muttered Jake.

Jody looked up at Mark. 'It's okay,' she said. 'I came to paint the back room anyhow. I'll paint and someone else can have my place. Bill is right.'

'Come on,' said Mr Benson impatiently. 'This isn't a

schoolroom. I don't need to waste my time while you diddle around.'

'Sorry,' said Mark. 'Okay, Bill, Roy and Al will work with you. The rest of you guys, let's divide up the other tasks. We need about five people on painting. The walls in the front north-east room need lining. We've got to start work on the stairs. They were almost completely ruined by the fire, and they have to be torn out so we can start again. The job requires top-notch carpentry. We need our best guys on that.'

'Robbie and I will paint,' said Jody decisively.

'Thanks,' whispered Robie. 'I was scared I'd have to learn how to make stairs, and with my luck they'd come out crooked.'

'I'd like to try my hand at working on the stairs,' said Jake.

'Okay,' said Mark, 'I'll work with you just as soon as I get them the paint.'

'I'll get it,' said Jody.

'No,' said Mark. 'I'm the only one who handles the paint. It's expensive and I keep it locked up in a closet. I'll bring you a can, and if you need another, ask me.'

'What am I going to do?' asked Mark's younger brother, Rudy. 'They told me I couldn't stay in there with the electrician.'

'You can help Jody and Robie,' said Mark. 'Jody and Robie, have you met my brother Rudy?' Rudy was about ten years old.

'Where have you been?' asked Jody. 'How come you haven't been around before?'

'I've been staying with my mom,' said Rudy. 'Hey, what did the mother ghost say to the baby ghost?'

'Bye,' said Mark, leaving the room.

'Nope,' said Rudy, 'she said, "don't spook until you're spooken to".'

Jody and Robie groaned.

Rudy turned out to be a sloppy painter, but a funny kid. He kept telling Jody riddles, only they were all ones that Jody and Robie had heard when they were ten years old.

'What's the last thing you eat before you die? You bite dust. . . . What did the burglar give his wife for her birthday? A stole. . . . What's the perfect cure for dandruff? Baldness. . . . What's green and dangerous? A thundering herd of pickles.'

After each punch line Jody and Robie groaned louder.

Jody couldn't take any more. 'Hey, Rudy,' she said, 'give us a break.'

'Sure,' said Rudy. 'What do you want? A broken leg or a broken arm.'

'Very funny,' warned Jody. 'Watch out, or I'll paint *you* instead of the wall.'

Jody paused. She looked very thoughtful for a moment. 'Can I ask you a serious question for a moment?' asked Jody. 'Does Mark stay with your mom sometimes?'

'Yeah. He sees her every summer,' said Rudy. 'But she and my dad are still always fighting and making digs at each other.'

'That's tough,' said Jody. 'We see our dad during the summer too. He and Mom get along okay, but it's still hard. He's got a new wife, and she's nice and all, but it's hard.'

'You know Mark started that other fire right when Mom and Dad were going through the worst of it. They were screaming at each other all the time. I was only a little kid, so they left me alone, but Mark got screamed at a lot, even though he didn't do nothing.'

'Does your mom know about Mark's arrest?' Jody asked.

'Yeah,' said Rudy, stirring the paint in the paint can and not meeting Jody's eyes. 'She called and Dad told her. She started screaming that it was all Dad's fault for letting him hang out with the Bullets.'

'Didn't she ever stop to think that he might not have done it?' asked Jody indignantly.

Rudy shook his head. He looked close to tears. 'The truth is that everybody seems to think he did it. You're about the only one I know who really doesn't.'

Jody put her arm around Rudy. 'You don't believe he did it, and neither do I,' she said. 'That makes two of us. I'm going to prove Mark innocent and you can help me.'

'How?' asked Rudy.

'Well, I made a list of people who I thought might be Mark's enemies,' said Jody, 'but you might know more.' She got her black-and-white-patterned notebook and showed it to Rudy. She had listed: Mary Aurelio, Joey Hennessey, Roy Washington, Ben Walker/Walker Construction, Bushmaster Enterprises???

'What's a bushmaster?' asked Rudy.

'It's a poisonous snake,' said Jody absent-mindedly. Suddenly her eyes lit up. 'Bushmaster . . . Bush . . . I wonder . . .'

'Wonder what?' asked Robie. 'What do snakes have to do with anything?'

'That's a good question,' said Jody. 'The bushmaster is one of the most deadly snakes in the world. It lives in South America, but I've got a feeling we've got one much closer to home, and it just might be the missing piece.'

17

A FLAMING WARNING

Jody stepped back to admire the wall they were painting. 'It's amazing what a coat of paint does,' she said. 'This room looks so much larger now that it's painted.'

Rudy put down his paint-brush and stepped back, and a smile crept across his face. 'It does look pretty good,' he said. 'Mark said this is going to be my very own bedroom – all to myself.'

'It's a great room,' said Robie. 'It's even got a nice view.' Robie stuck her head out the window.

'Careful of the paint,' warned Jody.

'WAIT A MINUTE!' shouted Robie. 'I SEE SMOKE!' She jerked her head back into the room so fast that she got a streak of white paint all over her hair.

'Smoke!' shouted Jody. 'Where?' She ran to the window. Rudy tried to get his head out the window, too, and all three of them were soon smudged with paint.

'See?' said Robie. 'It's around the corner of the house. It looks like it's outside on the street.'

'Maybe an automobile's on fire,' said Rudy.

Just then there was a shout from outside. Jody, Robie and Rudy ran through the house and out onto the porch. The rest of the gang joined them.

Jody's mouth fell open. She couldn't speak. She stared in wonderment. The smell of petrol and burning rubber stung her nostrils. Her bicycle was on fire!

'How can my bicycle be burning!?' shrieked Jody. The flames leaped around the wire spokes, twisting them so that they looked like overcooked spaghetti.

'Someone must have poured paraffin on it,' said Mark, moving next to Jody.

Jody's hand leaped to her mouth in involuntary horror. She took a step toward her bicycle. Mark put his hand out to stop her.

'Don't go near it,' he warned. He ran into the house and brought out his Ademco home fire extinguisher. 'Go pull the alarm on the corner,' he ordered. 'We should call the fire department even if I can put it out. It could spread or the wind could change.'

Mark held the heavy red extinguisher and pulled out the locking pin. He aimed the nozzle at the base of the fire.

Jake stood next to him. 'The flames are up higher,' he said.

'You always try to get the base of a fire,' shouted Mark, as the dry chemical powder shot over the wheels of the bicycle, sending up a stream of black smoke as the powder smothered the fire.

Within second the sirens of the fire engines could be heard, and two fire engines, a pumper and a ladder, screeched to a halt.

By then Mark had the fire completely under control. The fire fighters stared at the bicycle and NO PARKING sign which looked as if they had melted together.

'I don't believe this,' exclaimed Fireman Walker. 'Whose bike is this?' he asked.

Jody stepped forward. She was still in shock from the sight of the flames leaping around and through her bicycle. She stared down at the black mess that had been her bicycle.

Then she was seized by a coughing fit from the searing smell of burning rubber.

Mark led her to the side and put his arm around her shoulder as Jody tried to control her coughing. The firemen got out one of their hoses and hosed down the smouldering fire to make sure there was no flare-up.

'Take it easy,' whispered Mark. 'It's okay.'

'Okay?' exclaimed Jody angrily. 'Someone just destroyed my bicycle!' She coughed again.

'I know,' said Mark. He started to say something else, but Fireman Walker interrupted him. 'What in the world was this about?' he asked. 'That's the strangest fire I've ever seen in my life. Was this somebody's idea of a joke?'

'I don't know anything about it, honestly,' explained Mark. 'We were all working inside the house, cleaning up and fixing it up again. Suddenly one of the kids yelled and told me there was a fire outside. I couldn't believe we were having *another* fire. I ran outside, and Jody's bicycle was burning like some weird symbol. It was scary. I can't explain it. It looked somehow like one of those crosses that the Klu-Klux-Klan burns.' Mark's voice was shaking with anger as he spoke.

'That's what it reminded me of,' whispered Jody. 'I got chilled when I came out and saw it. It was one of the scariest moments of my life.'

Fireman Walker looked confused. 'Look, I've seen some strange things in my life, but this beats them all.'

'Hey, Ben!' shouted one of the firemen. 'Come and look at this.'

Fireman Walker walked over to the remains of Jody's bicycle.

'I should never have let you hang around here,' whispered Mark. 'It's too dangerous.'

'It's not your fault,' whispered Jody.

'Jody, Mark. Come and look at this,' shouted Ben Walker, motioning them over to him. He pointed to the spokes of Jody's wheels.

'Do you see that pattern,' he said. The fire had burned in a circular pattern around the spokes, almost as if it had been grotesquely decorated for a macabre Fourth of July. Burned threads of what looked like cloth were entwined in the wheels. With his heavy fireproof gloves Fireman Walker picked up one of the shreds. 'It smells of pure paraffin,' he said. 'Someone wound rags soaked in paraffin around the spokes.'

Mark swore under his breath.

'That's creepy,' whispered Jake.

'It's certainly a strange way to start a fire,' said Fireman Walker.

'Do we call in the fire masters on this one?' asked one of the firemen.

'Over a burnt bicycle?' Another fireman laughed.

Fireman Walker looked at Jody. 'There's too many coincidences,' he said. 'First you stopped by to ask about arson, about this very house,' he said. 'The next thing, we're called out because someone has set fire to your bicycle. If you ask me, someone doesn't like the fact that you're asking questions.'

'That's what I think, too,' said Jody.

Fireman Walker sighed. 'I'm going to call in a report to the master and the police, but they're overloaded with arson cases, and I doubt they're going to be able to give a burnt bicycle much attention. Nonetheless, I'd like you to be careful, young lady.'

'I will,' promised Jody.

The other firemen got back on their truck, and the driver started the engine. 'Come on, Ben,' shouted one. 'We've got to get back to the station.'

Ben was about to get back on the fire engine when he looked up at the porch and did a quick double take.

'Sam!' he said to the electrician. 'What are you doing here?'

'Trying to teach these young punks how to do their own wiring,' answered Sam Benson.

'Young punks,' muttered Mark under his breath.

'Oh, yeah,' said Ben. 'I forgot John had you still working over here. Did you see the fire?'

'Couldn't miss it,' said Sam. 'Never seen anything like that in my life.'

The driver of the fire engine honked his horn.

'I've got to go,' Ben said. He took Jody's hand. 'You keep in touch, you hear?' he ordered.

Jody nodded.

18

NO ORDINARY
PAINT CAN

Mark kicked at the smouldering remains of Jody's bicycle. 'How much did it cost?' he asked. 'I'll find a way to pay you back.'

'We'll worry about that later,' said Jody. 'Right now, we've got things to do.'

'What are you talking about?' demanded Mark. 'Jake, take her home. Someone is out to get you, and I don't want to be responsible. You and Jake and Robie, you'd all better get out of Northtown.'

'Great,' said Jody sarcastically. 'Is that how you want me to take this? Someone says "boo" and I run away.'

'I'd say burning your bicycle is a little more serious than saying boo,' said Jake. 'On a scale of one to ten, it ranks right up there.'

'I agree,' said Robie. 'I think we should leave it to the fire masters and the police.'

'Oh? And where exactly do you think they will rank a burnt bicycle on a scale of one to ten?' said Jody. 'You heard those firemen laugh when Ben even suggested calling the fire masters and the police. Besides, I'm not going home and that's that.'

'I wouldn't argue with her when she sounds like this,' Jake warned Mark.

Just then Sam, the electrician, came up to Mark. 'I've got to go now,' he said. 'First of all, I've got some other work to do, and second, all the kids are too excited over that fire to pay attention to anything else.'

'Yeah,' said Mark, 'I guess we are all a little upset. But thanks for coming.'

Sam nodded, got in his car and drove away quickly.

'All right,' said Jody. 'I want everyone to look around for a paraffin can. Whoever started the fire wouldn't want to be seen carrying the can for any longer than necessary. I think probably they hid it somewhere close by, and it's important that we find it.'

Mark nodded. He turned to the Bullets. 'Let's start looking,' he ordered.

'Oh, is little Jody Markson now the leader of the Bullets?' asked a mocking, familiar voice. 'I knew you were sissies, but this is getting to be a little too much.'

Mark whirled around to see Joey Hennessey with his arm possessively around Mary Aurelio. 'We heard the sirens and we had to come see if you were having another fireworks display,' taunted Joey. 'I've got to admit I never thought I'd see a bicycle in flames. It looked like a circus act.'

Mary unentwined her arm from Joey and took a step aside, as if to indicate that she didn't belong to Joey.

'Why don't you stay on your own turf?' demanded Mark.

'But such interesting things happen here,' said Joey, laughing.

'Get out of here, Hennessey,' warned Mark.

Suddenly Joey stopped smiling. 'I'll see you midnight, Saturday,' he warned.

'Are you coming, Mary?' he demanded.

Mary shook her head no.

'What're you doing?' demanded Joey. 'You waiting until Saturday to make up your mind?'

Mary didn't answer. Joey turned on his heels and left quickly.

'Come on,' said Jody impatiently. 'We've got to look for that paraffin can.' Jake followed Jody to the back of the house, and they poked around through some of the debris.

'Maybe I'll find another valuable paint can,' said Jake.

'If we find what I'm looking for, it's worth a lot more than money,' said Jody. 'It's worth Mark's freedom.'

'If you ask me, you don't have to look far to figure out who wants to scare you off,' insisted Jake.

Jody looked up from poking around through the rubbish in the backyard. 'Who?' she asked.

'Mary,' said Jake, 'that's who. She obviously doesn't like Mark paying so much attention to you.'

'But she broke up with Mark long before I came on the scene,' said Jody.

'Yeah, but she doesn't seem too happy about the break-up,' said Jake. 'Or haven't you noticed?'

'I've noticed,' said Jody. 'But it's hard to imagine her winding rags soaked in paraffin around my bicycle.'

'If you ask me, *that's* a sexist remark!' said Jake.

Jody blushed. 'I guess it was at that. Do you really think Mary did it?'

'She just happened to show up today, only minutes after it happened,' Jake pointed out. 'And besides, she was around on the day the first fire began. You yourself were the one to point out that she had broken up with Mark then. Why was she hanging around the house?'

'But she nearly started a riot when Mark was arrested,' said Jody.

'What better way to make sure that no one suspects her,'

93

said Jake. Suddenly Jake shouted 'WHOOPS!' as he stepped on a banana peel and almost fell on his head.

Jody giggled.

'You know, banana peels are really slippery,' complained Jake, catching his balance.

Jody laughed again. 'Yeah, and it's pretty funny when someone slips on one, too.'

'Ha! Ha!' said Jake.

Jody covered her mouth to keep from laughing. 'I'm sorry, but it really was funny.'

Jake picked up the banana peel and held it at arm's length. 'Yuk!' he said. 'I'm going to make sure nobody else steps on this.' He opened a dustbin to put it inside and suddenly shouted, 'Jody! This rubbish smells.'

'So what?' said Jody. 'All rubbish smells.'

'No, but this smells like paraffin,' said Jake. He peered into the can. Jody ran over. The dustbin was filled to the brim with green plastic rubbish bags, all closed tightly with wire ties.

'It must be inside one of those bags,' said Jody.

The dustbin was an oversized container used to dump materials when workmen were working. There were about five or six large green plastic bags in the bin.

'Let's get started,' said Jody. She untied the first rubbish bag and emptied it out. It was full of old coffee grounds, soggy remains of TV dinners and other things too disgusting to mention.

'No paraffin can,' said Jody.

'Yeah, but almost anything else you could mention,' said Jake.

'Let's put it back,' said Jody.

'We should have worn rubber gloves for this operation,' said Jake.

'Hey, Jody! Jake! What are you doing?' asked Mark.

'We're supposed to be cleaning up, not making a mess.'

'Jody's still looking for the paraffin can,' said Jake. 'We can smell it, but we can't see it.'

Mark came out, followed by Robie. 'Nobody found anything where we were looking.'

'Smell this rubbish,' said Jody. 'It reeks of paraffin.'

'I wouldn't smell this rubbish if I were you,' warned Jake.

Jody picked up the second green plastic bag. It was heavier than the first. She emptied it out. There were a number of large cans in the bag. 'Those are just the paint cans we've been using,' said Jody.

'Wait a minute,' said Jake. 'This bag smells even more like paraffin than the other.'

Jody picked up one of the cans. Paint had dripped over most of it, and she could barely make out the brand name of the paint they were using.

'It's an ordinary paint can,' said Mark.

Jody looked at it closely. She turned it upside down and showed it to them. The inside was clean as a whistle. The aluminium shone in the sun.

'There's something mighty peculiar about this paint can,' said Jody.

'It looks like an ordinary paint can to me,' said Robie.

Jody shook her head. 'You've seen our used paint cans. They're full of paint on the inside. Even if you try to get all the paint out, there's still some stuck to the sides, but the inside of this can gleams. Paraffin is a powerful paint remover, isn't it?'

Jake nodded his head.

Jody smiled at Mark. 'I think we've found out how your fingerprints got on that paraffin can,' she said. 'Come on, we've got to see Mom right now. Does anybody have a bicycle I can borrow?'

'You can borrow Rudy's,' volunteered Mark.

Rudy groaned.

Jake slapped him on the back. 'It's tough being a younger brother, isn't it?'

19

TRUST ME

The receptionist at Mrs Markson's law firm looked a little shocked when Jody arrived trailed by Jake, Mark and Robie.

'Uh, your mother's in conference,' she said, glancing around as if worried that some of the firm's paying clients might be upset by discovering what looked like a teenage gang in their reception room. Actually, Mrs Walters worried about respectability much more than did either Mrs Markson or any of her partners.

Mark picked up a magazine and slumped into a chair. Mrs Walters gave his clothes, including his 'Bullets' vest, a disapproving stare.

'Does your mother expect you?' she asked worriedly.

'No,' said Jody, 'but we've got something important to talk about. Mark is her client.'

'Oh,' said Mrs Walters with a sigh, and she turned to her desk.

'Mrs Walters is always worried that Mom doesn't take enough paying clients,' Jake whispered to Mark.

Mark nodded. 'Now I'm in debt to both your mother and your sister,' he said viciously.

'Hey,' whispered Jake, taken aback by the tone of Mark's

voice. 'I didn't mean you should take Mrs Walters personally. She treats everybody that way.'

'But it's true,' said Mark. 'I owe your mom because she's my lawyer and I can't pay her, and now I owe Jody because her bicycle got burned.'

'Why is that your fault?' demanded Jody. 'You can't take responsibility for everything. You didn't burn it.'

'How do you know?' Mark spat the words out. 'Everyone thinks I burned the house we were working on. What makes you so sure I didn't burn your bicycle too?' Mark's voice had started to rise and Mrs Walters stopped her typing and stared at him.

'Stop feeling sorry for yourself,' said Jody sharply.

'Sorry for myself!' shouted Mark. 'Is that what you think I'm doing?'

'What *are* you all doing here?' demanded Mrs Markson as she came out of her firm's conference room. 'What's all this shouting about?'

'I'm sorry, Mom,' said Jody. 'I didn't realise we were shouting. We've got to see you. I've got something important to show you.'

Mrs Markson glanced at Mrs Walters, who looked very upset. 'Why don't you all wait for me in my office,' said Mrs Markson, 'and get out of Mrs Walters' way.'

Mrs Walters looked up at Mrs Markson gratefully.

'Will you be long?' asked Jody.

'You sound like one of my demanding clients,' said Mrs Markson. 'But no . . . I should be able to finish this up. I'm just talking to a client and I'm almost through. I'll be with you in a few minutes.'

Jody led the way to her mother's office.

'I'm sorry,' said Mark when Jody closed the door. 'You were right. I guess I was feeling sorry for myself.'

'I shouldn't have yelled,' said Jody.

'You should have seen the look on Mrs Walters' face,' said Robie. 'She looked like she was going to have a fit.'

'She always looks like that,' said Jake. Jake sat down in the ultra-comfortable Herman Miller Ergon chair behind Mrs Markson's desk. He tilted it back, put his feet on the desk and stuck a pencil in his mouth. 'You may wonder why I've brought you all together,' he said in a pompous voice.

'You may wonder why you are about to get out of that chair so fast,' joked Mrs Markson, walking into her office. Jake quickly slid out of her chair.

'Whoops. Sorry, Mom,' he said. 'I was just warming up your chair for you.'

Mrs Markson laughed as she sat down in her chair. 'Okay, kids,' she said. 'What's this all about?'

'Mom,' asked Jody, 'have you actually seen the paraffin can that had Mark's fingerprints on it?'

'No, not with my own eyes. I did arrange for our own fingerprint expert to examine the can. Unfortunately, his conclusions concurred with the police's. The only fingerprints on it were Mark's. As you know,' said Mrs Markson, pausing to look Mark in the eye, 'our biggest problem is those fingerprints.'

'And I think I know how they got there,' said Jody, 'but I have to see the paraffin can first.'

'Can't you tell me about it?' asked Mrs Markson.

'I can,' said Jody, 'but it would be much better if I could show it to you. Is there any way we can go look at it now?'

'I suppose so,' said Mrs Markson. 'But –'

'It's really important, Mom,' said Jody. 'I think it'll make all the difference in Mark's case.'

Mrs Markson had learned to trust her daughter's hunches. She reached for the telephone and buzzed her secretary. 'Stacy,' she said, 'see if you can get me Milt Zucker at the D.A.'s office.'

Mrs Markson tapped her pencil on her desk impatiently. 'Milt,' she said after a few seconds, 'I'm glad I caught you in. It's Nan Markson. I want to come and examine the evidence in the Mark Brown case, particularly the paraffin can. Could I possibly see it right now. I could meet you at police headquarters. I'll be there in a few minutes. Oh, by the way, I'll have my investigating crew with me and also Mark Brown. I know it's unusual, but you haven't seen my investigators. I'll see you in a few minutes.' Mrs Markson hung up the phone. 'Come on,' she said. 'I'll tell Stacy and Mrs Walters to hold my calls.'

Mrs Markson drove them over to the district attorney's office, which was right above police headquarters. Mark squared his shoulders as they got out of the car. 'I hate going back in there,' he said.

'Trust me,' said Jody, but her stomach felt as if she had swallowed a Mexican jumping bean. She wasn't at all as confident as she sounded, that she could clear Mark. As they walked up the huge concrete steps of the massive building, Jody's pulse jumped as if she were running a marathon.

20

SWAMI O-HATAGO SIAM

Mrs Markson led them down a long marble hallway to the district attorney's office. Milt Zucker, a tall thin man with a receding hairline and an open smile, was waiting for her. He and Mrs Markson were often on opposing sides during a trial, but they respected each other.

'I've got the evidence on my desk,' he said. 'Come on in.' He looked at Jody and Jake. 'Are these your new fingerprint experts?' he asked.

'No, but they've become my experts on this case. This is my daughter, Jody, and my son, Jake, and you've met Mark Brown.'

Jody and Jake shook hands with Mr Zucker. Mark had his fists stuffed into his jeans' pockets and he didn't take them out.

Mr Zucker let them into his office. On top of his desk was a can with an official-looking tag on it, indicating that it was evidence. Jody took one look at the can and breathed a sigh of relief.

'I was right,' she said confidently. 'I know how Mark's fingerprints got on that can even though Mark didn't start the fire.'

The group gathered around the desk.

'Don't touch that can,' warned Mr Zucker.

Jody reached into a plastic bag she was carrying and showed them the paint can she had found. It was identical to the one on the desk. 'It's a paint can,' she said.

Milt Zucker shook his head. 'Of course. We knew that. But it reeked of paraffin. Obviously someone put the paraffin in the paint can.'

'But why?' Jody asked. 'Didn't you think to ask that question? Why would someone want to go to the trouble of putting paraffin, which is so dangerous, into a paint can?'

'What's your point?' Milt Zucker asked.

Jody ignored him. She turned to Mark, who was staring at the paint can. 'Mark,' she asked, 'what were you doing the day of the fire?'

'I was painting,' Mark said softly. 'We had just got the paint from the contractor – free paint. I wanted to make sure none of it got stolen, so I took it all out of the carton myself. Then I brought a can down and I started to paint.'

'But lots of people must have handled the paint can,' objected Mrs Markson.

Jody shook her head. 'No. Mark has a very elaborate procedure set up where he's the only one who handles the paint, I know, because Robie and I were painting today.'

Mrs Markson gave Mark a very thoughtful look. 'Why do you have such a particular way of taking care of the paint?'

'The people at Walker Construction told me to do it that way,' said Mark. 'They kept trying to impress me with what expensive paint they had given me, and that we couldn't waste it. They told me we wouldn't be able to get more.'

'Don't you see?' said Jody. 'Somebody was planning on setting up Mark practically from the beginning.'

Mrs Markson held up her hand. 'That will be enough for now, Jody,' she said, a warning tone in her voice.

Jody stopped in **mid-sentence**.

Mrs Markson held her hand out to Milt Zucker. He looked confused. 'We'll see you in court, Milt,' she said breezily, and then she practically herded Jody, Jake and Mark out the door.

'What's the matter, Mom?' asked Jody.

Mrs Markson shook her head. 'Nothing. I think you're really on to something, but I didn't want to give our whole strategy away to Milt before we came to trial.' Mrs Markson turned to Mark. 'Now, at least we have a reasonable explanation to give the jury as to how your fingerprints got on that can, but we need to know the motive.

'Money,' whispered Jody.

Mark looked at her as if she was crazy. 'That house isn't worth a thing,' he said.

'Don't be too sure,' said Jody. 'Mom, is there a way that you can find out if the house was insured?'

Mrs Markson nodded. 'You think that those papers at the Buildings Department didn't just happen to get lost,' said Mrs Markson, able to read her daughter's mind.

'Exactly,' said Jody.

'I'll go back to my office and see what I can dig up,' said Mrs Markson.

'Great,' said Jody. 'Meanwhile I've got some work to do for Saturday.'

'What's going on on Saturday?' asked Mark.

'The swa——' Mrs Markson started to say 'swap meet,' but before she could get the words out, Jody interrupted.

'The swami is coming for dinner,' said Jody. 'Mom has become interested in meditation and she's having a swami over for dinner, and Jake's going to cook a vegetarian meal. Aren't you, Jake? And I promised to shop for all the vegetables. Only I've been so busy, I haven't had a chance.' Jody's words tumbled out of her mouth.

Mrs Markson looked at Jody as if she had suddenly turned into a swami right before her eyes.

'Oh . . . that's right,' said Jake, realising that Jody didn't want Mark to know about the swap meet. 'We're cooking for your swami.' Jake winked at his mother over Mark's head.

Mrs Markson shook her head, but she reluctantly went along with it. 'Oh, that's right . . . Swami O-hat-a-go Siam.'

Jake giggled as he heard his mother. But Jody kicked him.

Mrs Markson smiled at Mark. 'Listen, Mark, don't worry,' she said reassuringly. 'For the first time I feel like we've got lucky on this case. I had put in a routine inquiry on the insurance, but now I'm going to follow it up. Right now, I've got to get back to the office.'

Mark shook Mrs Markson's hand. 'Thanks, Mrs Markson,' he said. 'I don't quite understand what's going on, but I'll trust you if you say it's good news.'

'Thanks, Mark,' said Mrs Markson, 'and don't worry about that swami stuff. It doesn't mean I've gone off the deep end. Meanwhile, you two,' said Mrs Markson turning deliberately to Jody and Jake, 'you stay out of trouble until you hear from me.'

Jody gave her mother an innocent look. 'Who? Me?' she asked.

Mrs Markson just shook her head.

Mark took the bus back to Northtown, and Jody and Jake were alone.

'Swami what a goose I am!' Jake laughed, doubling over and holding his stomach.

'I didn't want Mark to find out about the swap meet,' said Jody, but she started to laugh too. Finally, she stopped. 'Come on,' she said. 'We've got a lot of work to do this afternoon.'

'Hey, haven't we done enough?' protested Jake. 'Besides, you promised Mom you'd stay out of trouble.'

'If you remember,' said Jody. 'I didn't promise. All I said was "who me?"'

'You certainly *are* going to make a good lawyer someday,' said Jake admiringly.

'We're going to leave a calling card,' said Jody mysteriously, 'only we're not going to leave our names.'

21

JODY BAITS A TRAP

'Look for the word, "meet",' said Jody. She waved the scissors in her hand as she sat on the living room floor surrounded by scraps of newspapers. Chico and Groucho batted the strips of paper around with their paws.

'I got it in the sports section,' said Jake. 'Track meet.'

'Well, cut out the track and give me the meet,' said Jody.

'It sounds like a song,' said Jake.

'Come on, we're almost finished. Find me "midnight" and we're done,' said Jody.

'Hey, that sounds like another song, or at least a poem. You're writing poetry, aren't you?'

'Not exactly,' said Jody.

Jody had a blank sheet of typing paper in front of her, and she was carefully gluing bits and pieces of newspapers to it. Jake kept rifling through the papers looking for the word 'midnight'.

'This is much harder work than I ever realised,' said Jake. 'When you read about people sending notes from cut-up newspapers, they make it sound like any dumb criminal can do it. It takes a smart criminal.'

'Or at least one that's willing to take the time,' said Jody. 'We've been working for more than an hour.'

'Of course, you *would* insist on writing a long note,' said Jake.

'I wanted it to be subtle,' said Jody. 'Have you found "midnight", yet?'

'Wait a minute. . . . Here it is. It's in the food section . . . about some couple who has midnight dinners, only it's tiny.'

'You would be looking through the food section,' said Jody.

'Don't complain,' said Jake, handing Jody a tiny scrap of paper.

Jody looked around at the mess they were making. Harpo, Chico and Groucho had fallen asleep on the discarded newspapers.

Finally, she and Jake glued the last few words in place.

'Very poetic,' said Jake.

'If you were the person who committed arson, wouldn't you show up?' said Jody.

'I guess so,' said Jake.

'Let's go,' said Jody. 'We've got to deliver it.'

'I hope you know what you're doing,' warned Jake.

'I do too,' said Jody seriously.

After delivering their message, Jody went straight to the fire station and asked for Fireman Ben Walker. He was in the back playing gin rummy. He put down his cards when he saw Jody and Jake.

'Has something else happened?' he asked in a concerned voice.

'No,' said Jody, 'not really. We found a paraffin can in the back. It matched the can they found at the fire. We took it to the police.'

'Hey, Ben, you still concerned about that burning bicycle case?' joked one of the firemen.

if You Want to Find out

-who IS PAINTING The TOWN red

..COME TO the SWAP MEET.

'at ViCKerS Stadium. .at midnight

bring Flaming. red Paint ....

or El.se. /'LL' GO'

to The Police

Ben scowled. 'Did you come to tell me that?' he asked Jody.

'Yes,' said Jody. 'I also wanted to invite you to the swap meet we're having at Vickers Stadium tonight, at midnight, I hope you'll come.'

Ben looked at her curiously. 'A swap meet at midnight?' he repeated.

'Yes,' said Jody. 'I think it's important you be there. It could be a very hot time.'

'You're not being very clear,' complained Ben.

Just then the bells started to ring. Automatically Ben stopped talking and listened, five-seven-three.

'Eighteenth and Mercado,' shouted one of the fire fighters.

Ben pulled on his jacket and started to run toward the pumper. 'I'll be there,' he said over his shoulder.

Next Jody and Jake bicycled to the Bullets' house on Thornton Street. Rudy was sitting on the porch all alone.

'Where's everybody?' Jody asked.

'In the back-yard,' said Rudy. 'I'm keeping guard.'

'Guard?' asked Jody. 'Guard against what?'

'I'm supposed to look out to make sure none of the Razors come snooping around today,' explained Rudy. 'I wish I could be in the back with everybody else though.'

'What are they doing back there?' asked Jake.

'Batting practice,' giggled Rudy, 'only it's going to be the Razor's heads that get batted.'

Jody and Jake hurried through the house to the back-yard. Mark was standing in front of his gang, leading them through a series of karate exercises.

'HAI!' the gang shouted in unison as they thrust out one foot and leaned back onto the heel of the other foot.

Jody and Jake stared.

'HAI!' they shouted again, as with lightning speed they twirled around and now faced the back. Mark took them through the entire series, then he brought his feet together and bowed to the group. The gang bowed back.

Roy stepped out of line and glowered at Jody and Jake. 'This is no place for you,' he warned, taking a threatening step toward them.

'Roy is right,' said Mark. 'You shouldn't be here now.'

'Are you going to fight tonight?' Jody asked.

Mark nodded. 'I can't back down,' he said. 'There's nothing you can do to stop it.'

Jody didn't answer.

Even though it was Saturday, Mrs Markson spent the day at her office. She arrived home just about dinner-time. Jake had cooked a meat loaf, one of his favourite dishes. The whole house smelled wonderfully of meat juices and onion. Mrs Markson took a deep breath and sighed happily. 'I wonder if the swami is going to like meat loaf,' she asked as she walked into the kitchen. Jody was helping Jake make the salad.

'I made meat loaf in honour of Jody's swap meet tonight.'

Mrs Markson groaned. 'Can't we have the meat loaf without the puns?'

'Why did the crazy chef watch the lazy cow?' asked Jody.

'I don't think I want to know,' said Mrs Markson.

'He liked to watch the meat loaf,' answered Jody.

Both Mrs Markson and Jake groaned.

'You've been spending too much time with Rudy,' said Jake.

'Do you mean Mark's brother Rudy?' asked Mrs Markson.

'Right,' said Jody. 'He's a riddle freak. He can drive you crazy.'

'Speaking of being driven crazy,' said Mrs Markson, 'trying to track down the insurance on the Bullets' house on Thornton Street is not easy. Someone is being very careful to try to keep as much distance as possible between them and the insurance. There are about three different dummy corporations.'

'Was one of the companies Bushmaster Enterprises?' asked Jody.

Mrs Markson stared at her daughter. 'How did you know that?' she asked.

'I smelled a snake,' said Jody.

'I've got a riddle for you, Jody,' said Jake. 'How does the elephant get down from the tree?'

Jody pondered the question for a second. 'I don't know,' she admitted.

'He sits on a leaf and waits for the fall.'

Jody groaned. 'Why is that one for me?' she asked.

'Because if you ask me, that's what you're doing tonight.'

Mrs Markson gave her daughter a worried look.

22

A FLAMING END

The Marksons arrived at Vickers Stadium around eleven-thirty, but the place was already crowded. The huge sodium lights above the parking lot gave a yellow glow to the people setting up their card tables and milling around through the piles of books, records, souvenirs (almost all made in Hong Kong or Taiwan) and lots and lots of old clothes.

Mrs Markson parked and got out their card table. She started to set up some of their things. She turned to get Jody and Jake to help her, but they were staring at the crowd, examining it closely.

'Aren't you going to help?' complained Mrs Markson. 'This was your idea.'

'Right, Mom,' said Jody. 'We were just looking around.'

'Jake, you can't expect lightning to strike twice,' said Mrs Markson casually, and Jake jumped.

'What do you mean, Mom?' he asked.

'Don't expect to pick something up for a dollar and sell it for fifty dollars. Why did you jump?'

'Uh . . . lightning striking just sounded a little too close for comfort, especially with Jody's plan,' said Jake.

Mrs Markson looked confused.

'Never mind,' said Jody quickly, shooting her brother a

dirty look. 'Come on, Jake, help me bring out the stationary bicycle.'

When Jody got out of hearing of their mother, she grabbed her brother. 'You didn't have to jump at the word lightning,' she said.

'Lightning and fires are pretty close,' said Jake. 'Besides, you've got to admit your plan depends on lightning speed.'

'I know,' admitted Jody. They walked back to help their mother arrange their table.

Just then Kendra Ferguson came over. 'It's already a smash,' she said smilingly. 'People keep coming up and telling me that it's a unique idea. I want to thank you, Jody.'

While Mrs Markson was talking to Kendra, Jody casually said, 'Mom, do you mind if we take a look around.'

Mrs Markson smiled and waved them off.

'Let's go,' said Jody. Jake took an empty biscuit tin and put it in a large shopping bag. Then they set off.

Then Jake spotted Mr Walker and his partner, Mr Bush. Jake walked up to them smiling. 'Hi, Mr Walker,' he said. 'I've got another can for your collection. Wait till you see it.'

Mr Walker looked around the crowd nervously. 'I don't have time tonight,' he said sharply.

'But wait,' protested Jake. 'This is a beauty. You'll love it.'

'Look, kid,' said Mr Walker, not unkindly, 'I really can't talk right now.'

'But this will only take a minute; it's a beauty – in mint condition.'

'Okay . . . let me see it,' said Mr Walker.

Jake reached into the shopping bag and then seemed to drop it. Jody bent down to help him pick it up. The two of them seemed to fumble around for several seconds while Mr Walker stood on his side of the card table, continuing to look over the crowd as if he expected someone.

Finally Jake stood up. 'Here it is, sir,' he said, holding out his biscuit tin.

'That?' exclaimed Mr Walker.

'Right,' said Jake proudly. 'It doesn't have a dent in it.'

'But it's a biscuit tin,' said Mr Walker.

'Absolutely,' agreed Jake. 'A perfect biscuit tin.'

'It looks like you just bought it at a supermarket yesterday,' said Mr Walker in astonishment.

'Well . . . it's a little older than that,' said Jake.

'Get out of here, kid,' said Mr Walker. 'First of all, I collect paint cans, not biscuit tins.'

'Ahh . . . uh . . .' stammered Jake. He looked down at Jody who for some inexplicable reason had stayed down near the ground after Jake had dropped the shopping bag. Jody winked at Jake.

'Okay, Mr Walker, sir,' said Jake. 'Sorry I bothered you.' He picked up his shopping bag, and he and Jody left.

When they got out of Mr Walker's line of vision, Jake broke out into a sweat. 'I don't know why I ever go along with your plans,' he grumbled. 'Did you find it?'

Jody grinned. 'I did. It's in your shopping bag. Careful with it. It's full of paraffin. He must have been looking for a chance to plant it on whoever wrote that note. I'm sure he thinks Mark or one of the Bullets sent it.'

'He did seem nervous,' said Jake.

'Let's get rid of this paraffin,' said Jody. 'It's making *me* nervous. It's too dangerous to just leave around.'

Jody and Jake ran to the fire station across the street from Vickers Stadium. 'Is Fireman Walker here?' asked Jody.

'No,' said one of the firemen. 'He's over at the swap meet. Tonight is his night off.'

'Well, look,' said Jody, 'we found this can of paraffin. It's important evidence in an arson case. Will you keep it safe for us for a little while?'

'Look, young lady . . .' said the fireman, but before he could say more, Jody gave him the shopping bag, and she and Jake ran out and back to the swap meet.

Mrs Markson was still talking to Kendra Ferguson. All in all, Jody and Jake hadn't been gone more than ten minutes. An older lady came up to Kendra Ferguson just as Jody and Jake arrived.

'Kendra . . . I've been looking for you. It's such a wonderful idea to have this swap meet at night. Often in the afternoon, I get sunstroke, but this is kind of fun . . . it's so nice and coo——' The woman stopped in mid-sentence. 'My goodness,' she cried. 'What's that gang of teenagers doing at a swap meet?'

Jody and Jake whirled around. In the bright sodium lights, the Bullets and Razors stood out like menacing silhouettes from a grade-B movie. However, instead of fighting, the two gangs had stopped short, and they were staring at the friendly neighbourhood scene they saw in front of them.

Both gangs seemed to notice Jody and Jake at the same time. They looked at each other and then, as if one animal, they moved forward in a pack.

Jody and Jake walked up to meet them.

'What's going on here?' demanded Mark. Mark sounded as if he could barely control his fury.

'A swap meet,' said Jody sweetly. 'Did you guys come to swap something?'

'You know what we came for,' muttered Joey Hennessey under his breath. He turned to Mark. 'Did you have her arrange this, you yellow –'

'I'm not yellow,' said Mark angrily. 'You'll have your fight. Come on, we'll find another place. I didn't have anything to do with this.'

'Wait a minute,' commanded Jody. 'This is not an ordinary swap meet. If you stick around, you can watch us exchange a framed arsonist for the real arsonist.'

Mark's eyes narrowed as he heard her words. 'What are you talking about?' he whispered.

'If you postpone your stupid fight with the Razors, you can clear your name,' snapped Jody. 'But if it's more important for you to get into trouble, don't let me stop you.' Jody's frayed nerves were beginning to show. She knew her plan was dangerous, and she had had enough of the Razors and Bullets strutting around like peacocks.

'I'll say one thing for you, Jody Markson, you've got guts,' said Joey Hennessey. He stole a glance at Mark who still looked furious. 'Hey, cool down, Brown,' said Joey. 'She's right. I'd rather have you out of jail, so we can fight. If you got a chance to get out of this mess, you should take it.'

'And he's a Razor talking,' said Jody. 'Even *he* is smarter than you are.'

'All right, all right,' said Mark. 'You don't have to rub it in. What's your plan?'

'The plan is already in effect,' said Jody. 'We're just waiting for the final curtain.'

'Very dramatic,' said Mark. 'Now tell me what's going on.'

'I need a cigarette,' said Jody, ignoring his question.

Joey Hennessey reached into his pocket and handed one to Jody.

'You don't seem like the type to smoke,' said Mark suspiciously. 'I've never seen you smoke before.'

'Got a light?' asked Joey casually.

Jake took out a disposable lighter that he and Jody had bought just for this occasion. He held it up to Jody's cigarette.

Jody took a long drag and immediately started coughing and spluttering.

'Some cigarette smoker,' said Mark.

'This stuff's poison,' coughed Jody. 'I hate it. It's a killer. Nobody should smoke. They should outlaw cigarettes.'

'Thanks for the moral lesson,' said Joey sarcastically. 'First you bum a cigarette, and then you lecture me. Who needs it?'

'You should really quit smoking,' said Jody seriously, as she took another drag, then swallowed the smoke and started to gag.

'You'd make a great anti-smoking ad,' said Mark.

'Smoking is terrible for you,' repeated Jody. She took another drag. This time she didn't inhale. She just faked it, letting the smoke out quickly.

'What are you doing?' asked Mark impatiently.

'Believe me, I wouldn't smoke this cigarette if I didn't need it for my plan,' said Jody. 'And I'll never smoke another. Come on, let's go. Jake, you've got the can.'

'Are we gonna let this little twerp just order us around?' demanded Joey.

'We don't have much choice,' said Mark. 'She's the only one who seems to know what she's doing.'

'You'd better hope that's true,' said Jake. They followed Jody across the parking lot back to Mr Walker's table. He and Mr Bush were deep in conversation with Fireman Ben Walker. They all looked up in slight shock, as Jody and Jake and all the Bullets and Razors surrounded them.

'Mark! Jody!' cried Fireman Ben Walker. 'What are you doing here?'

Before anyone could answer, Jody turned to John Walker. 'It's midnight,' she said. 'We came to make a swap.' She reached into Jake's shopping bag and brought out a can of paint. 'You wanted to swap paint cans, didn't you?' asked Jody.

Mr Walker looked at the paint can. It was the same kind

that had contained paraffin and had been found with Mark's fingerprints.

'I don't collect those cans,' he said coolly.

'Oh, come on,' said Jody. 'I saw a can just like this under your table.' Before Mr Walker could react, she bent under the table and pulled out a paint can.

'I thought we could switch paint,' she said deliberately.

'I don't think so,' said John Walker, beginning to sound nervous.

'Why not?' she asked. Jody took the cigarette out of her mouth. 'Darn . . . my cig's gone out. Jake, give me a light.'

Jake took out the lighter and flicked on the flame. Mr Walker jumped as if he had received an electric shock.

Jody took the lighter from Jake and held it casually in her hand. 'Is anything wrong?' she asked. She leaned over the table, and accidentally brushed against the can she had taken from underneath Mr Walker's table. Then she seemed to casually drop her lighter.

'Ben, stop her! She's going to blow us up!' shrieked Mr Walker, as both he and Mr Bush backed away. But the Razors and the Bullets surrounded them and kept them close to the table.

Jody held the lit lighter close to the paint can.

'YOU FOOL! YOU'RE TRYING TO KILL US ALL!' yelled Mr Walker. His brother stared at him, his mouth hanging open.

Jody paused. Then she tipped the can all the way over, and white paint dribbled all over the card table.

'Paint, Mr Walker. It's paint, not paraffin. The paraffin is back at the fire department. They are keeping it safe for us until we get it to the police department as evidence. We switched cans earlier this evening when Jake came to sell you the biscuit tin. We wanted to make sure there were no more fires.'

Ben Walker looked as if he were in shock. 'Are you telling me my brother was responsible for arson?' he asked in a horrified voice.

'Yes,' said Jody softly. 'He and his partner, Mr Bush. They've got a dummy corporation called Bushmaster Enterprises. I guess they sub-consciously couldn't resist naming themselves after a snake. I put Mr Bush and Bushmaster together. I bet you'll find that a lot of buildings that have been torched belonged to Bushmaster.

'When Fireman Walker asked his brother to help Mark, Mr Bush and John Walker knew they had a foolproof plan. They had a friend at the Buildings Department who could make sure the papers were lost for a while. Even though they had abandoned the building, they still owned it on paper. Meanwhile, they insured it for far more than it was worth. They knew that with a teenage gang working there, it would be easy to blame them for arson. It was easy to get Mark's fingerprints on the paraffin can by simply filling an old paint can with paraffin.

'Everyone thinks gangs start fires just for fun. Nobody would have thought of looking further once they had arrested Mark.'

Jody looked at Fireman Walker. 'You were the one who helped me figure it out when you told me that most fires are caused for profit.'

'You always talked too much,' snarled John Walker to his brother. 'You never cared about money; all you cared about was your stupid job, a lousy fireman . . . making zilch. You make me sick.'

Ben Walker looked as if his brother had just physically punched him in the stomach.

'It's you who are sick!' shouted Jody. 'You endanger innocent people with your fires just to make money. I bet you had your electrician set fire to my bicycle to scare me away. I hope they put you away for a long time. I'm going to work with the police and help them get evidence. It'll be easy now that they know where to look.'

'Right,' said Jake. 'And don't come to our mom if you need a lawyer.'

'I wouldn't come to anybody in the Markson family if they were the last lawyers on earth,' snapped John Walker.

23

HOUSEWARMING, NOT BURNING

'Come on,' said Jody impatiently. 'We'll be late.' It was a crisp autumn day, and the Marksons were all in the kitchen watching Jake put the final touches on his mustard and herb chicken that he had grilled for the house-warming.

'This chicken can't be hurried,' said Jake.

'Why? Doesn't it want to get to the other side?' asked Jody.

'What do you call a greasy chicken?' asked Jake.

'A slick chick,' answered Jody.

Mrs Markson groaned. 'Oh no, I can't tell you how glad I am that the house is finally finished and maybe you'll be spending a little less time with Rudy.'

'Wait till you see it, Mom. It looks beautiful,' said Jody.

Just then, Harpo sat up and begged for a piece of the chicken.

'Sorry, Harpo,' said Jody, 'chicken's not good for you. But you're coming to the party. I'll bring some people biscuits for you and Fang.'

Joy brought out a box of dog biscuits in the shape of postmen, fire fighters and police officers.

'Just be sure Fang doesn't think that biscuit is Ben Walker,' said Jake.

'Don't worry,' said Jody. '**Fang** isn't really a bad dog once you get to know him.'

Jake finally finished his chicken and wrapped it in aluminium foil. Then Mrs Markson drove them to Northtown, to the Bullets' house on Thornton Street.

The front verandah had three coats of glossy white paint on it, and the Victorian trim on the top of the verandah was painted a beautiful robin's egg blue. The rest of the house was also painted white with blue trim. The verandah was full of people laughing and talking. Someone had set up speakers in the upstairs window, and jazz music soared out into the street.

'It's lovely,' said Mrs Markson. 'Whose idea was it to paint it white and blue?'

Jody looked a little sheepish.

'Was it yours?' asked Mrs Markson.

'Nope. It was Mary's, said Jake. 'But Jody was a good sport about it. She helped paint it.'

Rudy and his father came out on the porch and welcomed the Marksons. Mrs Markson shook Mark's father's hand. 'It's beautiful house,' she said.

'Thanks to you and Jody, it's ours now,' said Mr Brown. 'And Mark and the gang have got permission to fix up other houses in the neighbourhood for other families.'

'Yeah,' said Mark. 'Even the Razors are getting into the act.'

Ben Walker came walking up the sidewalk. He looked shy, but Mark jumped off the porch to greet him.

'Come on up,' said Mark. 'I'm so glad you came.'

Mrs Markson looked at Ben. 'It's been a tough year for him, what with his brother going to jail and everything, but I'm glad he came to the party. It took real guts.'

'I know,' said Jake, 'but he's got them. Remember, he's a fire fighter.'

'Hey, Jody,' interrupted Rudy, 'which is better: the house burned down, or the house burned up?'

Jody stared at Rudy in disbelief. 'Which is better?' she repeated.

'Neither!' said Rudy, grinning. 'They are both bad.'

'Yeah,' said Jody. 'I'll take a house*warming* over a house *burning* any day.'

Mark laughed. 'I agree,' he said.

If you've enjoyed this book, you may like to read some more Knight titles:

Elizabeth Levy

The Case of the Frightened Rockstar

Jody Markson is organising a rock concert to raise money to rebuild the school sports stadium, starring Michael Harper, a famous teenage rock musician and former student of the High School.

But a series of practical jokes, from red paint spilt over a batch of newly-printed posters to a mugging at the stadium, threatens to spoil all Jody's plans. It's as though someone wants to discourage her – in a most sinister and menacing way.

Another puzzle is Michael Harper himself – tense, nervous and frightened. 'It's as if I stumbled into quicksand,' said Jody. 'Everything about this concert seems treacherous, and I don't understand it.'

What can be behind it all? With only a few days to the concert, Jody and her brother Jake are determined to find out – and to expose the mysterious invisible joker.

Knight Books

Elizabeth Levy

The Case of the Counterfeit Race Horse

Jody and Jake are spending their summer holidays working at the stables attached to a nearby racecourse.

Jody loves horses, and she has a special way with a nervous and unhealthy racehorse named Pure Energy. But she is taken aback when after a short stay at the vet's, Pure Energy seems to make an astonishing recovery without her help.

Meanwhile, Jody experiences a succession of unfortunate 'accidents'. Mr Barrett, the stable owner, decides she is a liability and fires her. Torn between anger and disappointment, Jody is not sure what she misses more – the stables or Mr Barrett's son Peter.

Then when Pure Energy wins a surprising victory, and Mr Barrett is accused of fixing the race, Jody begins to suspect there's more to Pure Energy's performance than meets the eye.

Knight Books

Christobel Mattingley

The Jetty

The jetty is very important to the little South Australian community of Kanbi Bay, but it is under threat of demolition and closure. So everyone in the town is rallying to protest. Everyone except Brad.

Brad has always hated the jetty, but he has kept his feeling secret; not even his best friends Jenk and Johnno suspect how he really feels.

When a team of divers come to report on the jetty, the whole town anxiously awaits the result of their enquiry and Brad is in an awkward position – especially when he unexpectedly makes friends with the chief diver, Ian Fergus.

Knight Books

Nicholas Fisk

Leadfoot

'The Alvis was a noble old lady wearing a lop-eared hare on her bonnet . . . determined, wilful, handsome, upright, demanding and above all full of character.'

The 1926 Alvis 12/50 tourer belonged to Rob Lyle's father, but Rob longed for the day when he would be allowed to drive the old car himself. Secretly he dreamed of racing her at Brand's Hatch, willing her to victory, with the crowd shouting 'Leadfoot Lyle! Leadfoot Lyle!'

Then, one day while the family were on holiday in Scotland, the dream became a nightmare reality. Rob and his father had built a huge makeshift catapult, for fun, but it had suddenly collapsed, trapping Rob's father under a pile of beams and girders, and Rob knew the only way of getting help was to drive the Alvis – fast!

A fast-paced thriller, starring a very classy car.

Knight Books

More Exciting Knight Titles

ELIZABETH LEVY

☐ 28332 7 THE CASE OF THE FRIGHTENED
ROCKSTAR 95p

☐ 28333 5 THE CASE OF THE COUNTERFEIT
RACE HORSE 95p

CHRISTOBEL MATTINGLEY

☐ 26530 2 THE JETTY 85p

NICHOLAS FISK

☐ 26809 3 LEADFOOT 95p

*All these books are available at your local bookshop or newsagent, or can be ordered direct
from the publisher. Just tick the titles you want and fill in the form below.*

Prices and availability subject to change without notice.

KNIGHT BOOKS, P.O. Box 11, Falmouth, Cornwall.

Please send cheque or postal order, and allow the following for postage and
packing:

U.K. – 45p for one book, plus 20p for the second book, and 14p for each
additional book ordered up to a £1.63 maximum.

B.F.P.O. and EIRE – 45p for the first book, plus 20p for the second book,
and 14p per copy for the next 7 books, 8p per book thereafter.

OTHER OVERSEAS CUSTOMERS – 75p for the first book, plus 21p per
copy for each additional book.

Name ....

Address ....

....